COUNTRY WINEMAKING &
WINE COOKERY

COUNTRY WINEMAKING & WINE COOKERY

Muriel Hooker Mackay

David & Charles
Newton Abbot   London   North Pomfret (Vt)

Illustrations by Evelyn Bartlett

British Library Cataloguing in Publication Data

Mackay, Muriel Hooker
  Country winemaking & wine cookery.
  1. Wine and wine making—Amateurs' manuals
  I. Title
  641.8′ 72   TP548.2

ISBN 0-7153-8368-X

Typeset by Typesetters (Birmingham) Ltd
Printed in Great Britain
by A. Wheaton & Co. Ltd., Hennock Road, Exeter
for David & Charles (Publishers) Limited
Brunel House   Newton Abbot   Devon

Published in the United States of America
by David & Charles Inc
North Pomfret   Vermont 05053   USA

CONTENTS

	Acknowledgements	6
	Introduction	7
	Useful Weights and Measures	8
1	General Directions for Winemaking	9
	Winemaking Terms Old and New	32
2	Winemaking Recipes (in alphabetical order)	34
3	Mead, Beer, Cider, Cooking Wines and Vinegar	65
4	Liqueurs and Sundries	74
5	Syrups, Summer and Winter Drinks	84
6	Country Remedies and Herb Teas	100
7	Using Home-made Wines in Cookery	110
	Index	141

ACKNOWLEDGEMENTS

My grateful thanks are tendered to my daughter Sarah Carter, and to Richard Carter, for arranging my original manuscript into a typescript and encouraging me to offer it for publication; and also to all concerned in the production of this book.

INTRODUCTION

This book is written on the assumption that most people who take up winemaking do so in the first instance in order to save money. Certainly the fascination of making wine soon takes over and becomes an absorbing occupation in itself, and the drinking of it a pleasure and enhancement of day-to-day living; but economy of money and materials is usually the trigger to the process. I began it myself when, on taking over a neglected allotment, I saw that it was golden all over with dandelion flowers and couldn't bear the idea of wasting them.

There are numerous textbooks on winemaking in existence, but more and more frequently these seem to be based on the use of expensive apparatus and aids, and preparations from packets and tins. My aim is to return as far as possible to the old-fashioned methods by which many generations of cottage winemakers used the utensils and ingredients that were readily available at small or no expense, and produced highly drinkable wines containing none of the mysterious additives with which our modern diet is bedevilled.

Since prices and money values are constantly changing, there is no point in trying to give exact figures for the cost of each recipe, but a rough-and-ready method is to count the cost of a bottle of home-made wine as about that of 1lb (450g) of sugar. It takes about 8oz (230g) of sugar to make a bottle, the rest of the cost being that of the remaining ingredients, reckoning on getting fairly cheap fruit. If expensive fruit or juice concentrates are used the cost will be higher; if fruit is obtainable free from garden or hedgerow, or inexpensive vegetables or waste are used, it will be lower.

Finally, a few words of warning. Home-made wines are at least as alcoholic as French table wines, some are more so. They must be treated with respect, not swigged down by the tumblerful simply because they are there. Weak-willed people who cannot wait until their wine is properly matured and fit for drinking, or who are incapable of keeping any number of bottles unopened in the house, will either make themselves ill or become alcoholics, and should *never* become winemakers.

Never attempt distillation to make spirits. It is not only illegal but suicidally dangerous, as distillation produces concentrations of fusel oil, present only in tiny safe amounts in wine and disappearing during the maturing process. It can only be got rid of in distilled spirits by long maturing (at least three years) and other specialised processes. It is a poison which can bring about death, blindness, permanent mental derangement and other forms of brain damage.

USEFUL WEIGHTS AND MEASURES

Measurements in this book such as teaspoons, tablespoons, pints (in dry measure) and so on, always mean levelled-off, not heaped or rounded measure. By a tablespoon is meant a spoon of ⅔fl oz capacity (20ml/4 tsp).

In American recipes, always remember that a pint is not our Imperial pint (20fl oz), but 16fl oz, and so on throughout fluid measures. Also, an English tablespoon is four teaspoons, and an American tablespoon is three teaspoons.

FLUIDS

1 tsp	=	60 drops (5ml)
1 tbsp	=	4 tsp (20ml)
1pt	=	20fl oz (approx 0.6 litres)
1 quart	=	2pt (approx 1.2 litres)
1gal	=	4 quarts (approx 4.8 litres)

DRY WEIGHTS

2 tbsp	=	1oz (32g) sugar
8fl oz dry measure	=	½lb (approx 0.22kg) sugar
1gal fruit measure	=	approx 4lb (2kg) fruit
1 peck	=	2gal (approx 9.6 litres)
1 bushel	=	4 pecks (approx 38.4 litres)

1

GENERAL DIRECTIONS FOR WINEMAKING

INGREDIENTS

Extreme purists would tell you that the only ingredient proper to wine is the grape, which contains precisely the right proportions of sugar, water, pigmentation, natural flavour, tannic acid and (on the skin) natural yeasts to produce the perfect drink. However, in modern practice even the production of classical wines is not quite as simple as that, and in any case the word 'wine' at which the purists proudly point as actually meaning 'the fermented juice of the grape' can also be derived from the Greek *oinos* which means any fermented drink. The requirements of fermentation are sugar, water and yeast; to these should be added vegetable matter to provide flavour and colour, and a little tannin to assist both fermentation and flavour. Citric acid is also required where the vegetable content lacks it, which is why many country wine recipes contain orange or lemon juice, but where these are scarce two level teaspoonfuls of citric acid crystals per gallon (4.5 litres) of wine will do.

The finest country wines are those made from fruit or flowers, and pre-eminent among these are elderberry, blackberry, elderflower and gorse. They will be found to vary with the season and have vintage years just as grape wine does. Don't despair, however, if you have no garden or access to the countryside. Many excellent wines can be made from common vegetables such as parsnips or beetroot, and much that is usually regarded as waste, for instance the skin and seeds of marrows, fruit and vegetable peelings, even leftover rice pudding or leftover tea. In fact you can use virtually any vegetable matter as long as it isn't poisonous or of such obviously unsuitable flavour as onions or horseradish.

For those who, like me, never read a book from the beginning I would add a word of reassurance. If in your random dippings you have noticed expensive-seeming recipes such as mulberry, blackcurrant or peach wine, remember that these are cheap to those who have a tree or a soft-fruit patch, and don't think my words about saving money do not hold good. Very few people may have a mulberry tree, but quite a lot more have edible fruits which they don't think of using – ornamental quinces for instance, the fruit of the *Chaenomeles* or 'japonica', rose hips, windfall apples or pears. There is no need to use the choicest fruit or vegetables for wine, and overripe fruit is quite suitable as long as any brown rotten patches or signs of mildew or blight are completely removed. The cheapest oranges or grapefruit are as good as the dearest, and little apples, potatoes, carrots and the like, which would be too small or wizened for cooking or jam-making, still make good wine.

In the case of soft fruits, and especially blackberries, those which ripen earliest contain the most pectin and so the early ones are best for jelly, while the late ones where pectin is least are best for wine, since pectin can cause cloudiness. With dark fruits like blackberries, plums or elderberries a proportion of unripe red berries should be included to improve both colour and flavour. Otherwise it doesn't matter what stage of ripening has been reached, even overripeness to the point of squashiness. When gathering your own fruit, choose a dry sunny day as in picking for jam making.

Depending on circumstances, what is dear to one person is cheap to another. You may not be in a position to take advantage of such lavish old recipes as one I have which begins: 'Put a wheelbarrow load of rhubarb through the mangle . . .', but you may be handily placed for some big store in town where large sizes of the cheaper kinds of tinned fruit such as English rhubarb or plums are sometimes available at economical prices. Cut your coat to suit your cloth and your wine will be cheap, to mix a metaphor. The golden rule is not to miss your opportunities, and not to be afraid to experiment. For instance, marrows have been mentioned, but obviously pumpkins, squashes and melons come into the same category and can be home grown, or you may be offered the surplus from a friend's garden. Never say no!

The amount of vegetable material required is stated in each recipe, but a general guide is that wines of light body (mainly flower wines) need usually 1gal (4.5 litres) measure of flowers to 1gal (4.5 litres) of water; medium-bodied wines, usually fruit, require 4lb (1.8kg) of fruit to 1gal: and heavy wines of port type 6lb (2.75kg) or even 8lb (3.6kg) to 1gal. The corresponding amounts of sugar are about 3lb (1.4kg), 3½lb (1.6kg) and 4lb (1.8kg) respectively. Some old recipes are over-generous with sugar, leading to over-sweet wines; the amounts given in my recipes should be regarded as maximum, and some sugar may be saved by adding it in stages as described in the section 'Methods' in this chapter (p22). The least needed for a successful fermentation of 1gal (4.3 litres) is about 2½lb (1.1kg), unless grape juice or other sugar equivalents are used.

Granulated white sugar is the best kind of sugar for most recipes, and it is the cheapest. Occasionally a recipe may be improved by using Demerara, and this is always stated. Beware of soft brown sugars as their flavour is too strong. When in doubt, stick to white sugar and you can't do any harm. Golden syrup is used in a few recipes but, again, it affects the flavour and should not be used unless called for in the recipe.

Now the yeast. The process of fermentation consists of the breaking down of sugar by the yeast into alcohol, carbon dioxide and oxygen. The yeast cells require the oxygen in order to grow and multiply; as far as they are concerned the alcohol is a waste product and, when there is too much of it in their environment, they die. There is therefore a limit to the amount of alcohol that fermentation can produce. Furthermore, some strains of yeast can stand more concentration of alcohol than others. In French wines there is a special yeast strain for each type, and these can be bought and used with appropriate English fruits to get a wine approximating to the same type. There are also available 'general purpose wine yeast' tablets, but I have found in twenty-five years of winemaking that just as good results are given by ordinary baker's yeast, fresh if possible, but dried is quite good and easy to use.

It is possible to make wine without added yeast by making use of wild yeasts present on the fruit skins, but these yeasts die off at low concentrations of alcohol and do not produce very good wines. Baking or brewing yeasts are the strongest, so home-made wines tend to be stronger than the lighter French table wines.

For those who fancy matching the yeast to the type of brew and getting perhaps a better flavour, Sauternes or champagne yeasts suit all pale wines, Pommard yeast suits pinks and light reds, Bordeaux or Burgundy yeast darker reds, and port yeast sweet heavy brews.

There are also a number of additives on the market, the commonest being 'sulphite' as it is commonly called – sodium metabisulphite, best used in preparation in the form of Campden tablets. It is an invaluable steriliser for equipment, and can also be very useful as an ingredient, to stop a fermentation at a desired point and to help guard against the wine turning to vinegar. Fermentation can also be stopped by adding alcohol to kill off the yeast, which is why many old-fashioned recipes tell you to put in brandy when fermentation has died down. Other additives are sold as clearing agents, preventatives of haze, and as yeast nutrients. While having no special objection to their use I feel (in common with many others) that our food and drink today have so many additives, the long-term effects of which are really not known, that there is a strong argument against adding unnecessarily to their number. A slight haze in the wine almost invariably clears with time, and in any case does not affect the flavour at all – it is purely a matter of appearance, though naturally a bright, clear wine is to be preferred. But an incorrect use of an additive such as isinglass finings may even stabilise the cloudiness! Baked and crushed eggshells are safest and probably simplest if an additive must be used. The method is to drop 1tsp of these into each cloudy bottle and leave it until it clears, and then draw off the wine into a clean bottle for storing.

As to nutrient tablets, the old-fashioned nutrient was a slice of toast on which the yeast was spread, and it is still as good as any of the more modern methods.

Other additions to various wines which may be found in recipe books are such things as Barbados sugar, black treacle, liquorice and similar strong-flavoured substances, all of which should be treated with the utmost caution and in my view are better not used at all as they can ruin the flavour of your wine. To get a warmth in the wine, peppercorns, mustard seeds, ginger or cloves are sometimes recommended. Of these I find ginger and cloves much the safest, and if used in the right amount their presence becomes undetectable after a few months. Always beware of recipes which call for several ounces to the gallon — this is far too much! A piece of ginger no bigger than a Brazil nut, and/or six or eight cloves, is just about the right amount.

Acid in some form, as has already been mentioned, is an essential ingredient. Citrus fruits supply it, as also does citric acid or, if nothing else is available, strong tea. Tannic acid as well as citric acid is actually desirable; tea supplies this, and can always be added where a modern recipe calls for the additive grape tannin. About half a teacup of strong tea or teapot drainings to the gallon is right.

The final ingredient not to be forgotten is water. Some people like to use distilled or boiled water, but tap water is perfectly all right provided it is normally drinkable and well-flavoured. If it happens, for instance, to be heavily chlorinated it would be best to boil it. The finest wine can be made with fresh, unpolluted deep spring water, but few of us are lucky enough to have it readily available.

13

EQUIPMENT

Since the great recent upsurge of interest in home winemaking, a large range of equipment has appeared on the market. Some of it is excellent and useful, some quite unnecessary. The stages of winemaking normally require a vessel in which to make the mash, or must, that is a mixture of fruit pulp and water; vessels in which to ferment and mature the wine; and bottles in which to store it. Also required is some kind of equipment for syphoning wine from one vessel to another, and for straining it.

A plastic bucket will do for the first; any large glass or pottery jar for the second, provided it has a narrow neck; second-hand wine bottles or even 'fizzy pop' bottles for the third. A nylon funnel, 1yd (1m) length of plastic tubing, and a piece of muslin or thin nylon curtaining are also required. For stirring the wine an 18in (45cm) length of strong wooden dowelling is ideal.

It will be seen that specially-made bins, demijohns, and various other pieces of apparatus are not essential. However, it is fair to say that gallon glass wine-jars, or demijohns, are very well worth having as they can be fitted with pierced corks and airlocks (plastic ones are not expensive) and this removes some of the worry from the fermentation stage of the wine, an airlock being the best protection against the dreaded vinegar bug. Nevertheless, seven-pound sweet jars or the like are very good for fermenting if carefully covered with four layers of cotton cloth tightly tied around the neck or held with a rubber band.

The old-time cottage winemaker sometimes possessed an oak tub for mashing and oak casks for fermenting and storage, and these are unexcelled in the unlikely event that you have any, and are prepared to undertake their cleansing and the making of the rather large quantities of wine needed to fill them. Otherwise the cottager used any vessel to hand – bread crocks, salters, toilet ewers, glass or glazed pottery jars. You can ferment your wine in two vessels if one isn't large enough, and any of the foregoing are suitable provided you are sure no flavour or residue of any kind remains from previous uses. Never use for wine anything which has contained vinegar.

Plastic containers such as may have held fruit juice or squash are quite suitable for the short-term processes, mashing and fermenting, and for short-term storage. In every case the neck or opening must be suitable for covering as described above, or plugging with a cottonwool plug; avoid wide or awkwardly shaped openings. The plastic should be white or colourless.

For covering mash tubs an old large tablecloth or old well-washed curtain will be quite suitable as long as it is perfectly clean and can be folded in four and still come well down the sides of the tub.

The one absolutely forbidden thing is anything made of metal. From start to finish, wine must not be put in metal containers or touched with metal spoons. Wooden spoons, very well scrubbed, a wooden stick or one's own hand (when no heat is involved) are the best things for stirring. In recipes where ingredients are boiled an enamel saucepan should be used. (Stainless steel pans or even aluminium may be used for boiling ingredients if enamel pans are not available, but enamel is always preferable, especially if acid fruits are involved. A covered oven-glass or ovenware casserole used in a slow oven is also good for extracting juice.)

As to bottles, this is a point where my advice is not entirely orthodox. The experts insist that only proper wine bottles are suitable; but although agreeing that they are desirable, I would say it is better to have makeshift bottles than no wine! Well-washed pop bottles with screw caps are quite usable, if you make sure that the metal inside of the cap is protected by a card or plastic lining. Squash or fruit juice bottles can also be used, but as they are thin you must be quite sure fermentation has ceased before bottling or you might get burst bottles. One Campden tablet to 1gal (4.5 litres) should ensure success.

Again, straight-sided wine bottle corks are the only orthodox thing to use, but if you are using makeshift bottles these corks are often unsuitable and instead you should use cork stoppers and keep the bottles upright instead of storing them on their sides. If you attempt any sparkling wine recipes it is essential to use strong bottles. Champagne bottles, cider flagons, beer or ginger beer bottles will do, ordinary wine bottles will not. They must have screw tops or corks must be tied down.

You can buy a cork-flogger to hit the corks into the bottles, but a few blows from a mallet or an old-fashioned solid wood rolling pin will do just as well. Similarly, cork squeezers can be bought, but ordinary nutcrackers will do the job.

When the boiling of ingredients is called for, you may not have a pan large enough to boil 1gal (4.5 litres) or more, but there is nothing against dividing the material into batches. As previously stated, enamelled pans are best, but non-stick pans are also suitable.

Useful though not essential items are a bottle-drainer, which can be made at home with dowelling pegs inserted in a board, and a fruit-crusher of wood like an old-fashioned potato masher or vegetable presser.

Making a bottle drainer for twelve bottles

Materials
Two pieces of wood 24 × 4 × ¾in (73 × 10 × 2cm)
39in (99cm) of ½in (1cm) dowelling
Wooden batten 27 × 2 × ¾in (69 × 5 × 2cm)
Waterproof glue

Cut the batten into three lengths, each measuring 9in (23cm), and cut the dowelling into 3½in (9cm) lengths

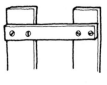

Screw one piece of batten across one end of the wood slats, and two thicknesses across the other end to give a slope for drainage, leaving 1in (2.5cm) between lengths

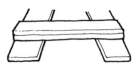

Make six holes at 4in (10cm) intervals down the middle of each slat. Drill at an angle, so that when the pegs are inserted they slope slightly backwards, as shown. Glue them in with waterproof glue

Finally, remember that all containers should be slightly larger than the nominal amount they will have to contain; for instance a mashing tub or bucket for 1gal (4.5 litres) of wine should be of 1½–2gal (7–9 litres) capacity so as to contain the water and the fruit or flowers and in some recipes the sugar, and still leave a space of 2–3in (5–8cm) at the top. Fermenting jars should have an additional capacity of about 1pt per gallon (600ml per 4.5 litres) to allow for frothing up in fermentation. On the other hand the spare space should not exceed these amounts – for instance, don't ferment 1gal in a 2gal jar, or too much air will get into the yeast and you will not get a proper fermentation.

It is extremely helpful to make markers on the outside of your fermenting jar or demijohn at the levels of 6pt (3.5 litres) 7pt (4 litres) and 8pt (4.5 litres). Do this by pouring in measured amounts of water and marking where it comes to with coloured adhesive tape. It saves time and trouble later.

METHODS

Winemaking is simple, and there are only slight variations in the method of preparation according to the nature of the fruit, flower, herb or juice which forms its basis. There are, however, two questions almost always asked by beginners – 'How long must I wait before I drink the wine?' and 'Can I make something sparkling like champagne?'

To the first question I would say shortly, 'Six months or more.' People are always trying to find out a way to hasten maturing. I was myself given a recipe by an expert, an official of a Winemaking Union and a chemist by profession, to hasten the production of an apple wine by using tinned juice and adding crystal malt. The result was to be 'drinkable in three weeks'. It may have been drinkable dietetically, but according to the palate was no better than firewater. The same applies to tins of prepared concentrated juice labelled 'Ready in three weeks' (or six weeks, or even three months). It all depends on one's definition of drinkable, but the improvement in all these wines when kept for six months is dramatic, and I think it best to make up one's mind to this from the start. The process of maturation is a mysterious one, involving the tiny changes, imperceptible currents, and gradual integration and blending of all the flavours in the wine to produce an inimitable result. No use to try to hurry it. If you simply must have something quick, try a fruit beer such as apple beer, lemon ginger beer or elderflower lemonade, but remember these are not wines and won't keep long.

The second question is partly answered in the previous paragraph; elderflower lemonade is sometimes inaccurately called elderflower champagne because of its delicious flavour and fizziness. There are also recipes for sparkling home-made wines but all suffer from the fact that, to get the sparkle, carbon dioxide must be dissolved in the wine under pressure, so that it will rush out as bubbles when the wine is poured out. This in turn means that the wine must ferment rapidly in the bottle to set up the internal pressures to dissolve the gas. Therefore, it throws a sediment of dead yeast cells to the bottom of the bottle and this breaks up when pouring and clouds the wine unless it can all be poured off rapidly in one go as must be done with home-bottled beer for the same reason. Commercially, there are ways around this. In the famous *méthode champenoise* (the only way of making true champagne) the bottles are turned upside down at a particular stage of fermentation so that the sediment goes into the neck. When it is settled there the necks are frozen in a bed of ice, the bottles turned right way up once more, the cork and its now adhering plug of sediment withdrawn, the bottle instantly topped up with reserve wine, corked and tied down. Otherwise, sparkling wines are made by the *cuvée close* method, that is fermenting in a sealed vat from which the wine is drawn into a second sealed chamber leaving the lees behind. There is also the cheap (and nasty) *vin mousseux* which is made by pumping in carbon dioxide under pressure, like fizzy pop.

It will be seen that none of these methods is very simple or easy for the home winemaker. However, there is a happy phenomenon of winemaking which sometimes gives the amateur a bonus in the form of a semi-sparkle in the wine, sometimes called *pétillance*, which can be very delightful. This is the malolactic ferment, a secondary fermentation which used to be said to appear in the wine at the flowering time of the flower or fruit of which it was made. This is now generally agreed to be a superstition, and warm weather is thought responsible. Some authorities regard it as a fault or 'disease' in the wine; I prefer to look on it as a gift from the fates.

Preparation
Returning to actual preparation methods, these can be briefly tabulated as:

(1) Preparing a mash with boiling water.
(2) Preparing a mash with cold water.
(3) Extracting juice by boiling.
(4) Some old-fashioned wines are first fermented in the mash tub. This is always stated in the recipes.

Boiling should never be carried on for longer than stated in the recipe, as over-boiling fruit leads to the extraction of pectin and an obstinate haze in the wine. Furthermore, an old winemaking adage says, 'Boiling water sets a red, but spoils a yellow.' With few exceptions this is true, and the more delicately flavoured wines, which are usually light in colour, can have flavour and bouquet largely removed by boiling water.

For **method 1** make sure your plastic bucket or other mashing tub is absolutely clean. Look over the fruit, pick out any leaves, twigs, etc, and if it seems at all dirty or gritty give it a quick wash under running water. Put it in the bucket and pour over it the required amount of boiling water. Handling large quantities of boiling water can be hazardous and it is best divided among several pans, or else use a kettle boiled up several times in succession. Alternatively, if you have a really large enamel boiler, you can boil up the water in it, tip in the fruit, and bale the mash into the bucket when it has cooled enough to handle.

Cover the bucket immediately; if it has a lid, put on the lid and throw a tea towel over it, otherwise put on your four-fold cotton cloth and tie with string or fasten with a large rubber band. If there is any danger of the cloth sagging into the liquid,

19

Covering the mash tub

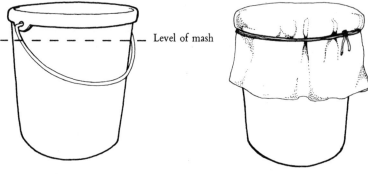

Level of mash

Plastic bucket

Put on the lid, and cover with a tea towel held in place with string or a strong rubber band

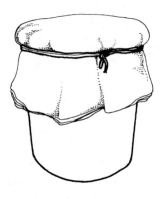

If there is no lid, cover with four layers of cotton cloth and tie closely with string or a rubber band

For wide, squat mash tubs, put two sticks tied in a cross on top before covering with the cloth

put two sticks tied together in cross form on top of the bucket under the cloth. The cloth must remain clean and dry throughout or it will not function to protect the wine.

For **method 2** proceed similarly but using cold water. In each case, stir and squeeze the mash daily with your hands or a wooden crusher for as long as stated in the recipe, or until you feel all possible goodness has been extracted from the ingredients.

Straining the mash

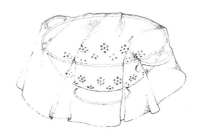

Line a colander with close-mesh nylon curtaining (about a yard square)

Place the colander in the top of a large enamel pan or crock, and pour the liquid through

Squeeze the remainder of the mash by twisting the curtaining

21

A week to ten days, or even longer, may be required. Remove immediately any mildewed material which may develop.

Scald your straining cloth of muslin or nylon and then strain and squeeze the mash into a clean bucket or bowl. Have a good big cloth, abut a yard (one metre) square is right, so that you can gather it up and squeeze the fruit by twisting the cloth. Cloudiness at this stage doesn't matter, it is not like jelly-making. More important is to get the utmost drop from the fruit. When all is strained, cover the bowl or bucket carefully while you prepare the yeast.

If you are using a wine yeast, follow the directions on the tube of tablets. In the case of fresh or dried brewers' yeast, cream it with 1tsp of sugar, stir in ¼pt (150ml) lukewarm water, put it into a clean bottle or small jar and bung the neck with cotton-wool, and set it aside to froth up. This method gives the best start to your fermentation, but it is possible if you are hurried simply to sprinkle dried yeast or a broken-up tablet into the top of the fermenting jar. Where a recipe calls for yeast spread on toast, fresh yeast can be spread on directly; dried yeast is creamed with sugar and a little lukewarm water and then spread.

Now have ready a fermenting jar and put into it through a dry funnel about two thirds of the required sugar. Pour in enough of the strained mash to dissolve the sugar, stirring with the dowelling stick. Add more liquid to make up to the 6pt (3.5 litres) mark, add the yeast and lemon juice, tea or any similar ingredients required by the recipe. Put in an airlock and set in a warm place (70°F, 21°C). If any mash is left over, put it in a clean wine bottle with 2 or 3oz (60–90g) of sugar and a pinch of yeast, put a cottonwool plug in the neck and keep it beside the fermenting jar to use for topping-up. The first violence of the fermentation dies down in three or four days and the spare wine can then be added to reach the 7pt (4 litres) mark.

When the fermentation has gone on for about ten days, add half the remaining requirement of sugar. To avoid a great uprush and commotion in the wine, syphon off about 1pt (600ml), dissolve the sugar in it and pour it back slowly through the funnel. Refit the airlock. After another week repeat the process with the remaining sugar. Experience will show you whether you can save a little sugar at this stage, using say a total of 2¾lb (1.25kg) in a 3lb (1.4kg) recipe. After adding the final sugar, make up the wine in the jar to about half an inch (12mm) above the 8pt (4.5 litres) mark, to allow for wastage in bottling; if no spare wine is left, top up with cool boiled water.

For **method 3** once your boiled extract has cooled and been strained, proceed as before.

The wine will now go on fermenting quickly for a month or so, and one advantage of using an airlock is that you can see exactly what is happening. At first the bubbles come through every second or so; then they slow down gradually, until by the time there is only an occasional bubble, perhaps half-hourly, the wine is ready for bottling. I have seen it recommended to bottle wine when the bubbles are reduced to about one a minute, but I think this would be asking for blown corks or even burst bottles. What may be done at this stage is to rack the wine into a clean demijohn, especially if it has thrown a thick layer of sediment, and to bottle it after another couple of months. Alternatively, if on tasting the wine seems dry enough, you can stop the fermentation with one Campden tablet and bottle after two or three days; or you can bottle it in strong bottles if you want a sparkling wine.

If you are not using airlocks you must depend on judging by eye, looking for small bubbles which collect and disperse on the surface, movement in the wine which can be seen when some fragment from the lees rises and sinks in the jar, or tiny bubbles rising when the jar is tapped sharply. If the container is opaque and there is no airlock, the ear has to be the judge, listening for a faint hissing.

Although the wine may now be bottled, there is a great advantage in racking it into a large jar or a clean demijohn and storing it in a cool place for up to six months before bottling. What is called the insensible fermentation takes place during this time, improving the clarity and flavour of the wine. Some wine-makers believe in several rackings. It should not need an airlock at this stage but can be corked or bunged. Do not leave it resting on the lees without racking as this can lead to a musty flavour.

Bottling

As with everything used in winemaking, bottles must be spotlessly clean. Some people believe in cleaning absolutely everything with Campden solution, but this should not be necessary unless some utensil or container is particularly suspect. Thorough cleansing with detergent or soda in the water, extremely thorough rinsing and (in the case of bottles) drying off in a cool oven, should ensure that no bacteria or vinegar spores remain. Corks should be boiled, or soaked for half an hour in Campden solution (two tablets to 1pt [600ml] of cold water). No rinsing is required when Campden solution is used.

Place the demijohn of wine on a table and have beside it a lower table or a kitchen chair or stool on which to stand the

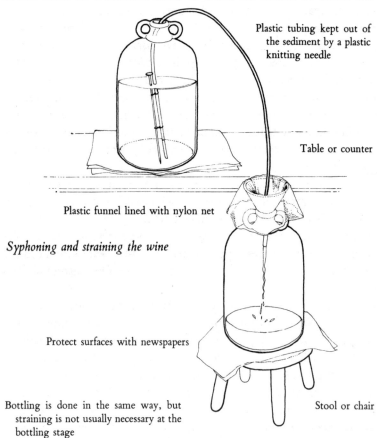

Plastic tubing kept out of the sediment by a plastic knitting needle

Table or counter

Plastic funnel lined with nylon net

Syphoning and straining the wine

Protect surfaces with newspapers

Bottling is done in the same way, but straining is not usually necessary at the bottling stage

Stool or chair

bottles. A good thick wad of newspaper protects the surfaces on which you work. Few people can bottle wine without spilling just a little. Have ready some plugs of cottonwool or tissue as temporary stoppers. Make sure the length of plastic tubing is perfectly clean inside and out. Take out the airlock and cork and push the end of the tubing down into the demijohn. A good tip to make sure the end of the tube doesn't go right into the sediment is to fasten a plastic knitting needle or a wooden skewer to it with two rubber bands, leaving 1in (2.5cm) projecting beyond the end of the tube. Suck the tube until you get a mouthful of wine, put your finger over the end of the tube, and then insert it carefully into the neck of the bottle waiting on the lower level. The wine will syphon off into the bottle. Equipment can be bought for starting and stopping the flow, but sucking and using the finger are not unhygienic if practised by a clean and healthy winemaker. Conversely, in the event of suitable tubing being unobtainable, racking may be done by careful pouring.

When the wine comes near the neck, withdraw the tube carefully, close end with finger, put the bottle aside with the other hand, and put the next bottle in place. As the wine nears the bottom of the demijohn tilt it carefully to keep the end of the tube covered and get the maximum amount of wine out.

Put a cottonwool or tissue plug in each bottle top while you get ready to put corks in. About 1½in (3.8cm) of air space should be left at the top of each bottle neck.

Put the bottle to be corked on a very firm surface – I usually use the floor! Take a cork and squeeze the end with nutcrackers or cork squeezer to start it in the bottle neck. Make sure it is straight, and then drive it in with a few hard sharp blows with your mallet, rolling pin or flogger. Some people can't get the knack, and then a good way is to put the end of the cork against a wall and push with a twisting motion. The top of the cork should be as nearly as possible level with the neck of the bottle. Cork stoppers are much easier to put in, but bottles so corked cannot be stored on their sides. Anything meant for long keeping should always be corked with the conventional wine cork and later sealed with wax. For appearance it can be capped with foil

Take a piece of string 18in (45.5cm) long, and double it in half

Tie a knot 1in (2.5cm) from the end to form a loop

Place the string around the bottle neck, and tie it in a reef knot opposite the loop

Bring the loop up and thread one end of the string through it

Pull tight, and tie the two ends in another reef knot

View from above

also. Label the bottles with name of wine and date of vintage or, if you like, of bottling before storing in a cool dark place – about 50°F, 10°C is right, if possible.

Wine which is destined to be kept for several years for some family celebration or the like must be treated with the respect given to ancient port or Madeira. Storage on its side is essential to keep the cork moist and avoid any danger of mouldiness.

Remember the wine will probably throw a sediment, so about a week before it is required the bottles should be stood upright to get it settled to the bottom. Two hours before it is to be drunk, bring the wine out without shaking or disturbance and decant it carefully. Have a source of light behind the bottle so that the instant any cloudiness reaches the base of the neck decanting can be stopped, the bottle being instantly, but with steady hand, raised from the mouth of the decanter. Stopper and keep in dining room temperature until required.

The last half-bottle or so of wine from a large jar may be very cloudy and full of sediment. It is worth pouring this into a spare bottle and, after letting the sediment settle, racking off the top into a small bottle for cooking use.

ADDITIONAL NOTES

Fitting airlocks
Plastic airlocks (the cheapest, and quite satisfactory) are made in two components and glass ones (longer lasting unless accidentally broken, and sterilisable by boiling) in one. Both have a projecting tube at the bottom to go through a cork. Pierced corks to fit standard sizes of jar are cheaply bought. Pierced rubber bungs are also quite good. If using cork, soak it for an hour or so in Campden solution or boiled water and then push the airlock in until it is well seated. Fit the cork carefully to the jar, pressing well in. Pour a little boiled water or Campden solution into the outer part of the airlock (if plastic) to about halfway up the sides, and then put in the top component making sure it is sitting properly. In the case of a glass airlock, pour in the liquid until it is halfway up both bubbles. As soon as the wine begins to ferment you can see at once if your airlock is working by the breaking bubbles of gas. If it doesn't work, check over the fitting until it does. For maturing, when the airlock has to stay in place for some time, a little paraffin wax can be run around the cork. A bad fit can be corrected by wedging with cotton wool. Check the water level frequently and top up as needed. Keep airlocks and necks of jars clean. A good tip is to invert a plastic bag over the whole airlock when fitted.

Fitting the airlock to the demijohn

Make sure that the airlock is well-seated and that the cork fits tightly

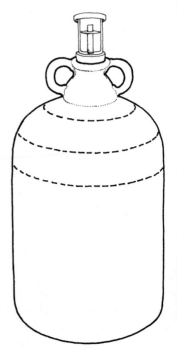

Liquid level after topping up for maturing

Liquid level after adding extra sugar

Liquid level for fast fermentation

Plastic airlock

Upper component

Fit the lower component into a pierced cork or rubber bung

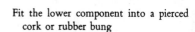

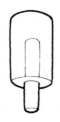

Lower component

Fix it to the neck of the demijohn. Pour in water or Campden solution to about halfway up the airlock. Put on the top component. The water level in the outer sleeve should at once rise, and shortly afterwards bubbles of gas will be released through the lock

Glass airlock

Fit the airlock to the bung, and ease it carefully into the neck of the demijohn. Pour in water or Campden solution to about halfway up both 'bubbles'

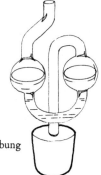

Cork or rubber bung

Covering fermentation jars without an airlock

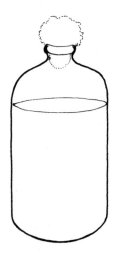

If wide-necked, eg confectionery jar, cover it with four layers of cotton cloth tightly tied or held in place with a rubber band

If narrow-necked, squeeze a handful of cotton wool in to make a good bung, as shown

Use of Campden tablets

The various uses of Campden tablets are referred to in the text and recipes, but to recapitulate:

(1) They are of great use (though not essential) in cleaning fruit and in controlling fermentation. The usual strength is one tablet to 1gal (4.5 litres), simply dropped in the wine, crushed first if you like.

(2) A solution of two tablets to 1pt (600ml) water is the best steriliser for equipment, needing no rinsing. It is good for use in airlocks and for wiping over airlocks and jars in use. For cleaning large jars a pint or two swilled round the already washed jar and then left standing in the bottom until the jar is required, is perfectly adequate – no need to be extravagant with quantities.

Remember, cold water must be used. In warm or hot water the sterilising qualities are released too fast to be effective.

Where Campden tablets are not available a good safe cleanser is ordinary bicarbonate of soda solution – 2tsp to 1pt (600ml) water.

(3) If unwanted yeasts are suspected in the must, put in one or two tablets per gallon (4.5 litres) 24 hours before adding yeast.

(4) To prevent oxidation of light-coloured wines ('Madeirisation'), add one tablet per gallon (4.5 litres) to the finished wine.

Disasters

Strangely enough the most dreaded disaster of the home-wine-maker, the turning of the wine to vinegar, is in a sense not a disaster at all, since the vinegar itself can be used. The only really irrevocable disasters are the breakage of a bottle or jar (or in the old days, the leaking away of wine through the defective cask or bung) and the contamination of the wine by bacteria, when it becomes thick and jelly-like and nothing can be done to save it. This is, however, a very rare occurrence, due to a failure at some point of the absolute cleanliness rule. Turning to vinegar, in spite of all precautions, is rather more common, due to the great prevalence of the vinegar spores, the so-called 'bug', which are carried in the air and also by fruit flies. Hence the care necessary in covering wine at all stages, using airlocks where possible, and only exposing wine to the air for the shortest possible time at any stage.

If the must (mash) becomes noticeably vinegary, you can decide whether to throw it away or not; but if the vinegar smell and taste are only noticeable after adding the sugar you may as well allow it to ferment right out and then bottle it for use as wine vinegar. Bramble wine becomes an excellent vinegar, equivalent to the best red wine vinegar; elderberry also, although it retains some elderberry flavour, but it is very good for all beef dishes and, with sugar and hot water, is a good cold cure. Not only are such vinegars good in cooking, but they serve for all the usual household uses of vinegar, for instance in furniture polishes and for cleaning brass and copper. It may be a little risky to use it in pickles and chutney as the strength is not known.

Another trouble is an intractably sweet and sickly wine. Long keeping will sometimes improve matters, and the same applies to crabbed and bitter wines. It may prove possible to blend a sweet with a too-dry wine and get excellent results; perhaps the same wine in successive years or even two different wines (eg bramble and apple) used as a blend. If all else fails, a really undrinkable wine can usually be used in cooking with complete success.

'Corking', the imparting to wine of the flavour of a mildewed cork and the origin of that little 'tasting' ceremony in restaurants, is not curable, but is avoided by careful sterilisation and good corking and storage.

Once again – it can't be said too often – Nature makes the wine. The winemaker's job is to ensure sterile or near-sterile cleanliness of all equipment, and exclusion of air as much as possible in processing – otherwise Nature is just as happy to make vinegar.

WINEMAKING TERMS
OLD AND NEW

Barm Liquid yeast formerly obtainable from brewers. In using old recipes, substitute appropriate amount of yeast.

Blinking *See* **Sticking**. 'To blink' is archaic for 'to go to sleep'.

Campden sterilising solution 2 Campden tablets to 1pt (600ml) cold water.

Campden tablets A preparation in tablet form of sodium metabisulphite and citric acid.

Fermentation Active stage of wine shortly after addition of yeast. Breaking down of sugar by yeast into alcohol and carbon dioxide.

Fermenting to a finish Allowing the fermentation to die down completely before storing the wine to mature.

Fining Improving the clarity of the wine by filters or additives, eg isinglass.

Fortifying a wine This is the strengthening of the alcohol content by adding spirits. Brandy is the most often recommended in recipes but in many cases is not essential and vodka or aqua vitae may be used instead, both being cheaper than brandy and flavourless, which may be an advantage.

Fretting A too-slow fermentation usually caused by too low a temperature.

Going to sleep *See* **Sticking**.

Grey Hen Old name for stoneware fermenting jar, sometimes with a tap.

Insensible fermentation First stage of maturing, after fermentation has apparently stopped.

Lees The thick muddy deposit at the bottom of wine vessels, consisting mainly of dead yeast cells.

Mash *See* **Must**.

Must Crushed fruit or mixture of ingredients in water; first stage of winemaking.

Proving Mixing and activating the yeast before use.

Putting together Preparing the must.

Racking To rack wine is to transfer it from one container to another, leaving behind the lees. Racking may be done by pouring, syphoning, or drawing off by a tap.

Sticking A fermentation sticks, or stops too soon, if the temperature is too low or (rarely) too high, or if the must is lacking in sugar, acid or nitrogenous matter (nutrient). It can also stop if there is too much sugar due to an unbalanced recipe, and in this case adding a little water may be the remedy.

Yeast does not act under 40°F, 4°C or over 80°F, 26°C. Moving the wine to a warmer or cooler position should first be tried, check the sugar content and acid content and remedy if out of balance, finally if lack of nitrogen seems to be the cause add a yeast nutrient tablet, a slice of bread, or ½tsp of Marmite extract per gallon (4.5 litres).

Sulphiting The addition to wine of sodium metabisulphite or Campden tablets to sterilise wild yeasts or bacteria or to control fermentation.

Syphoning A process based on the axiom that water finds its own level, by which, if a liquid is drawn upwards from a vessel by suction or pumping and if the tube then bends downwards, the liquid will continue to flow as long as the level of liquid in the receiving vessel is below the level in the first vessel.

Tartar A hard deposit on the inside of old barrels and sometimes of old decanters, caused by the solidification of the sedimentary deposits of the wine.

Tops and bottoms This phrase sometimes occurs in old books and refers to the belief that the first and last wine drawn from a cask is inferior in quality (for instance, the first three and last three gallons in a twelve-gallon cask). Fermenting in demijohns does not produce this problem!

2

WINEMAKING RECIPES

Apple Wine

1pt (600ml) tinned pure apple juice (not concentrate)
Juice of 1 lemon or 1fl oz (30ml) lemon juice
Water to make up to total 1gal (4.5 litres)
3lb (1.4kg) sugar
2tsp dried yeast

Mix the apple juice and lemon juice and make up to 1gal (4.5 litres) with cold water. Stir in 2lb (900g) of the sugar, put in fermenting jar and add the yeast. Add the rest of the sugar in stages over a fortnight. Ferment to a finish, rack and bottle at once (it will be clear because the fruit juice is clear to begin with). Ready in 3 months but better kept for 6.

Apricot Wine

6lb (2.75kg) fresh apricots
1gal (4.5 litres) water
4lb (1.8kg) sugar
1oz (30g) yeast

Put the apricots in a bucket and pour on the water, cold. Cover well. Squeeze and stir daily for 10 days. Strain on to sugar in fermenting jar, add yeast, ferment for 16 days, rack and strain into clean jar and move to cooler place, ferment to a finish, bottle and keep for 9 months.

Balm Wine

This wine is made with lemon balm, *Melissa officinalis*, some-times mistakenly called lemon verbena. The latter is a tender shrub, *Lippia citriodora*, rather rare and not what is required. Lemon balm is a hardy and vigorous herbaceous perennial and the best time to make wine is in early July before it flowers. The first time I made this wine was from a recipe which began, 'Take a good bunch of balm . . .' and alas, my idea of a good bunch was not the author's, and the wine turned out very pale and what this family calls 'mere'.

2 quarts (2.25 litres) balm leaves, picked off the stems before measuring	2½lb (1.1kg) loaf sugar
	2 lemons, thinly peeled
	White of an egg
1gal (4.5 litres) water	1oz (30g) yeast on slice of toast

Boil the water with the sugar and the juice of the lemons and egg white beaten in, for 45 minutes, skimming well (use 2 or 3 pans if necessary). Put the balm leaves and lemon peel in mashing tub, pour on the boiling liquid and stir frequently until it is almost cold. Float the toast with the yeast on top, cover and ferment for 3 days. Strain into fermenting jar and ferment to a finish. Rack, strain, store for 3 months, strain into bottles. Keep 6 months before use. Said to be a good tonic.

Banana Wine

It sometimes happens that greengrocers sell overripe or blemished bananas cheaply, and it then pays to make this wine. It is extremely rough when young but becomes very good in 18 months to 2 years.

4lb (1.8kg) bananas (after peeling)	2¾lb (1.25kg) sugar
4oz (110g) sultanas	Juice of 2 lemons
1gal (4.5 litres) water (cold)	1oz (30g) yeast

Soak the bananas, sultanas and one or two of the banana skins, if in good condition, in the water for 3 or 4 days, well covered, stirring and squeezing daily. Strain on to sugar, add lemon juice, put in demijohn and add yeast, ferment to a finish. Rack, store, bottle after 3 months and keep at least 18 months.

Beetroot Claret: *see* **Romany Claret**

Beetroot Wine

4lb (1.8kg) beetroot
Water
3lb (1.4kg) sugar
2 lemons

Piece of root ginger the size of a
   hazelnut
6 cloves
½oz (15g) yeast

Clean the beetroot and cut it up quickly into a pan. Cover with
water, bring to boil and simmer for twenty minutes. Strain off
the liquor and make it up to 1gal (4.5 litres), if necessary, with
cold water. When it is lukewarm, mix in 2lb (900g) sugar, the
thinly peeled rind and juice of the lemons, ginger, cloves and
yeast. Put in fermenting jar, ferment for a week, then add
another ½lb (230g) sugar. After 3 more days add the rest of the
sugar. After 4 weeks rack into jar with airlock. Ferment to a
finish, rack, store and bottle as usual. Keep at least 9 months.

Bilberry Wine: *see* **Whortleberry**

Blackberry and Grape Claret

2½lb (1.1kg) blackberries
6pt (3.5 litres) boiling water
18oz (500g or ½ can) Light Red
   grape juice concentrate (claret
   type)

1 tsp citric acid
A little cold tea
Burgundy yeast
1½lb (680g) sugar
1 Campden tablet

Wash, drain and crush the blackberries. Pour on 6pt (3.5 litres)
boiling water. When cool, add grape juice concentrate, citric
acid, 2 tbsp cold tea, and the yeast. Ferment for 5 days. Strain
and squeeze on to the sugar in a demijohn. Top up with cold
boiled water and fit airlock. Ferment to a finish. Strain into clean
demijohn, add a Campden tablet, stopper and store for 2
months. Bottle and keep 4 months or longer.

This makes a very fine dry wine similar to Médoc and is well
worth the cost (about one quarter that of a cheap commercial
wine).

Blackberry Wine: *see* **Bramble**

Blackcurrant Wine

4lb (1.8kg) blackcurrants
1gal (4.5 litres) water
4lb (1.8kg) sugar

1oz (30g) yeast on a thick slice of toast

Strip blackcurrants from stalks with a dinner fork into mashing tub. Crush with a wooden spoon or vegetable presser. Pour the boiling water over them, cover and stand for a week stirring daily. Strain on to the sugar in fermenting jar, mix well, add yeast on toast (if the jar has a narrow neck, cut toast in cubes). Ferment 14 days, rack and strain into clean jar, ferment to a finish, store and bottle as usual. Keep at least a year.

See also **Redcurrant and White Currant Wines**

Bramble Wine

6lb (2.75kg) blackberries
1gal (4.5 litres) boiling water

3lb (1.4kg) sugar
1oz (30g) yeast on a slice of toast

Wash, drain and crush the blackberries. Pour the boiling water over them, cover and stand for 10 days, stirring and squeezing daily. Strain on to sugar in fermenting jar. Add the yeast on toast, cut up if necessary to pass through the neck of the jar. Ferment for 3 weeks, rack and strain into a clean jar, keep 3 months and then bottle.

An optional addition to this recipe, which enhances the flavour, is about 8oz (230g) ripe sloes mixed in with the blackberries. It is a quick-maturing wine and in some seasons is drinkable by the Christmas of the year it is made, but it is best kept about 9 months. If you can pick blackberries from the hedgerows this is the cheapest of all wines (requiring no additives) and one of the best. Don't be tempted to boil the berries even a little or you will get a jam flavour.

Bramble Tip Wine

1 gal (4.5 litres) tips of bramble shoots (taken when young and tender)

1gal (4.5 litres) water
3lb (1.4kg) sugar
¾oz (22g) baker's yeast

Cover the bramble tips with water and bring to the boil. Simmer for 10 minutes. Cool, strain, and make up to 1gal (4.5 litres) with water. Put in a demijohn with the sugar and yeast, ferment to a finish, rack, store and bottle as usual. Ready for use in 12 months.

Bramble Blossom Wine

1gal (4.5 litres) blackberry
  blossom
1gal (4.5 litres) water
1 gill (150ml) brandy

1½lb (680g) sugar to each gallon
  (4.5 litres) of liquor
½oz (15g) yeast

Boil up the water and when it has cooled pour it over the blossoms. Add yeast, stir well, cover and leave for a week, stirring and squeezing daily. Then strain and squeeze on to the sugar in a demijohn. Ferment to a finish, rack, add brandy and

store for 6 months. Two to three days before bottling remove cork and replace with airlock. Bottle and keep 3 months at least.

Broom Wine

1gal (4.5 litres) broom flowers (no stalks)	Rind and juice of 2 lemons and 2 oranges
1gal (4.5 litres) water	3lb (1.4kg) preserving sugar
	1oz (30g) yeast

Put the thinly peeled rinds into the water, add the sugar, stir and boil all together for 30 minutes. Allow to cool; when just lukewarm pour it over the flowers and add the lemon and orange juice. Stir in the yeast, ferment 3 days, then strain into fermenting jar. Make up to 1gal (4.5 litres) with water if necessary. After 10 days rack and store. Bottle off after 2–3 months and keep 6 months.

Bullace Wine

Bullaces are the fruit of the wild plum, *Prunus insititia*, which flowers a little later than the blackthorn or sloe (*Prunus spinosa*) and has larger fruits. In West Cornwall where I live the fruit is called bullens or Kea plums, after a district where they flourish.

4lb (1.8kg) bullaces	1lb (450g) Demerara sugar
1gal (4.5 litres) water	½oz (15g) baker's yeast
2½lb (1.1kg) white sugar	1lb (450g) raisins

Wash, drain and crush the bullaces, pour on the boiling water and leave 3–4 days, stirring daily. Stir in the sugar and add the yeast. Cover and leave another 3–4 days. Strain into a fermenting jar and add the raisins, chopped small. Ferment to a finish. Strain and store 3 months before bottling. Keep 8 or 9 months.

Carnation Wine: *see* Mrs Sinkins

Carrot Wine

4lb (1.8kg) carrots	8oz (230g) sugar to each pint (600ml) of liquid
1gal (4.5 litres) water	
2 oranges and 2 lemons	1oz (30g) yeast

Scrub the carrots well but do not peel. Cut into ½in (12mm) slices. Simmer in the water until very tender. Strain and measure the liquid. Put the sugar and the oranges and lemons, scrubbed and sliced, into a wide-necked jar. Pour on the hot carrot water and stir until sugar is dissolved. When lukewarm add yeast, ferment 14 days and then rack into clean fermenting jar. Ferment to a finish, rack, store and bottle. Keep at least 6 months.

Celery Wine

This uses the outside stalks of celery and is said to be very good for rheumatism sufferers. If you can only make a little at a time, ferment in small jars and mix the batches together when you have enough to make 1gal (4.5 litres), so that you can store it in bulk.

Outside celery stalks	Demerara sugar
Water	Yeast

To each 1lb (450g) of celery allow 1 quart (1.2 litres) water and boil until tender. Strain off the liquid, measure and add sugar in the proportion of 3lb (1.4kg) to 1gal (4.5 litres). When lukewarm, add yeast spread on toast in the proportion of ½oz (15g) to 1gal (4.5 litres) or equivalent dried yeast creamed and spread. Ferment to a finish, rack, store and bottle. Use after 1 year.

Champagnes: *see* **Garden** (gooseberry), **Grapefruit, Rhubarb** and **White Currant.** *See also* **Elderflower Lemonade (p89)**

Cider Wine: *see* **Pomona**

Clarets: *see* **Blackberry and Grape Claret** and **Romany Claret**

Clover Wine

4lb (1.8kg) clover blooms	2 lemons
1gal (4.5 litres) water, boiling	2 oranges
3lb (1.4kg) sugar	1oz (30g) yeast on toast

Gather the clover (either red or white), weigh the blooms, then spread them in the sun for the rest of the day to wilt. This improves the flavour.

Now put them in the mashing tub and pour on the boiling water. When lukewarm add sugar, lemons and oranges sliced, and yeast. Ferment for 5 days, stirring daily. Strain into demijohn. After 5 more days rack and strain into a clean jar and ferment for a fortnight. Move to a cooler place for a week or two, then rack, strain, store and bottle as usual. Keep at least 6 months.

Coltsfoot Wine

Coltsfoot is such a cheering spring flower. I've seen it even growing all over mine tips in the Midlands before anything else took root, and the yellow blossoms brighten the dullest day or place. It is a famous medicinal herb and so the wine should be good for you!

Pick and measure the flowers on a sunny day and then spread on sheets of paper in an airy room to dry. They may be used after 2–3 days or completely dried and stored in paper bags (labelled 'Coltsfoot flowers to make 1gal wine') for future use.

2 quarts (2.25 litres) coltsfoot flower heads (measured when fresh)	2 lemons
	3lb (1.4kg) sugar
	1gal (4.5 litres) water
2 oranges	1oz (30g) yeast on toast

Put in mashing tub the flowers and the sliced fruit. Boil the sugar in the water for 10 minutes, pour over the flowers while hot. When lukewarm float the toast with the yeast on top. Ferment for 21 days. Strain into jar and ferment to a finish. Rack, strain, store and bottle, keep for 6 months.

Country Wine

This is for using up odds and ends such as overripe or otherwise surplus fruit from the garden, pulp from jam-making or syrup-making, leftovers of stewed fruit or fruit fillings, etc.

8lb (3.6kg) mixed fruits	3lb (1.4kg) sugar
Water to 1gal (4.5 litres)	½oz (15g) yeast

Put all the whole fruit in a mashing tub and just cover with water. Add leftovers as available. Stir and squeeze daily until you have the required amount, up to about a fortnight. Keep the amount of water as low as possible. Strain and measure the juice and make up to 1gal (4.5 litres) with cold water if necessary. Stir in sugar, put in fermenting jar, add yeast and ferment to a finish, rack, store and bottle. Keep at least 9 months.

Cowslip Wine

It's hard to imagine that there are still places where these lovely flowers grow profusely enough to be turned into wine, but if you know of such, good luck to you.

1gal (4.5 litres) cowslip heads	½oz (15g) yeast or a champagne
1gal (4.5 litres) cold water	yeast tablet
4lb (1.8kg) sugar	

Use the whole flower head but no fleshy stalks. Soak the flowers in the water for a fortnight, watching for and removing any decayed flowers. Strain and squeeze on to the sugar in fermenting jar, add yeast, ferment 14 days. Rack and strain, ferment to a finish but taste at intervals for sweetness and stop fermentation with a Campden tablet at required point. Rack, strain, store and bottle as usual. Keep for a year.

Crab Apple Wine

The fruit of either wild or ornamental crab apples can be used for this wine.

1gal (4.5 litres) crab apples, sliced	3lb (1.4kg) Demerara sugar
1gal (4.5 litres) water	1oz (30g) yeast (optional)

Put the sliced crab apples into the water in a bucket, cover well and soak for a fortnight, squeezing every few days. Strain on to the sugar. Cover and leave for 4–5 days, stirring daily. It should ferment spontaneously after about 2 days, but yeast can be added if you prefer. Strain again into fermenting jar. Ferment to a finish, rack and store 3 months before bottling. Keep 9 months or longer.

Currant Wine (Red and/or White)

½gal (2.25 litres) red or white currants, or mixture of both
2lb (900g) sugar

1gal (4.5 litres) water
1 wineglass sherry
1 small wineglass brandy

Gather the currants on a dry day, string and crush them, measure after crushing. Add water and sugar in the above proportions, stir well, ferment for 3–4 days, stirring daily. Strain into jar with airlock, ferment to a finish, rack into clean jar, add sherry and brandy, store for 6 months before bottling. Keep at least 3 months in bottle.

For a red or white currant wine without sherry or brandy, follow the recipe for blackcurrant wine.

Damson Wine *(rich old-fashioned)*

8lb (3.6kg) damsons
1gal (4.5 litres) boiling water
3lb (1.4kg) sugar per gallon (4.5 litres) of juice

½oz (15g) baker's yeast or port yeast

Put fruit in bucket, crush well, pour on boiling water, stand 21 days stirring and squeezing daily. Strain, measure, add sugar and yeast. Keep skimmed for 2–3 weeks then strain into fermenting jar and ferment to a finish. Bottle and keep at least 1 year, 2 years for preference when it will resemble port.

Dandelion Wine *(sweet)*

3 quarts (3.5 litres) dandelion heads (no stalk)
1gal (4.5 litres) of water
3½lb (1.6kg) Demerara sugar
1 orange

1 lemon
½oz (15g) bruised root ginger
8oz (230g) raisins
½oz (15g) baker's yeast

Pick the dandelions in sunshine when the flowers are open. Put the flowers in mashing tub, pour on the water, boiling. Stand for 3 days, stirring daily. Strain into a pan, add sugar, thinly peeled rinds of fruit, and ginger. Bring to the boil and simmer for 20 minutes, keeping up the volume of water by adding a little boiled water from time to time. Cool, strain into fermenting jar, add raisins and fruit juices. Add the yeast and ferment to a finish. Rack, store, bottle and keep for 1 year.

Elderberry Wine

Gather the elderberries as complete heads but without any thick main stalk and measure, allowing 1gal (4.5 litres) heads to 1gal (4.5 litres) water. Alternatively strip the berries off with a dinner fork before measuring and allow 2 quarts (2.5 litres) of berries to 1gal (4.5 litres) water.

1gal (4.5 litres) elderberries on stem, or 2 quarts (2.5 litres) stripped
1gal (4.5 litres) water
3lb (1.4kg) sugar
2 tbsp strong tea

A lump of ginger and a few cloves
1oz (30g) baker's yeast or Burgundy yeast
Slice of lightly browned toast

Strip the berries from the stems and put in a large pan. Add as much of the water as the pan will take, bring to the boil and boil for 20 minutes, and when cool enough to handle strain on to the sugar and mix well. Put into a fermenting jar, add the tea, ginger, and 6–8 cloves, make up with water to make 1gal (4.5 litres) finished wine. When lukewarm add the yeast spread on

44

toast. Ferment for 3–4 weeks. Rack into clean jar and let it ferment to a finish. Bottle after 2–3 months. Keep for at least a year, it becomes very good after 18 months to 2 years.

See also **Raisin and Elderberry Wine** *(port-like)*

Elderberry Port

Elderberry juice
12oz (350g) sugar to each quart (1.2 litres) of juice

8oz (230g) chopped raisins to each quart (1.2 litres) of juice

Pick the elderberries when they are mingled black and red, to get the best colour. Strip them and put the berries in a jar or casserole. Heat the jar in a pan of hot water, or by placing well covered in a slow oven, until all the juice is drawn from the berries. Strain and measure the juice, and if necessary set aside in a jar with cover or airlock while another batch is made, until you have the desired amount.

Add the sugar and raisins in the above proportions and stir well. Ferment for 3 weeks, skim, strain and store. Bottle after 3 months, keep 1 year.

Elderflower Wine
Important note: Measuring elderflowers
A winemaking beginner who tried elderflower as her first wine, used to shudder at the name thereafter. Reading '1pt elderflowers', she had painstakingly stripped the tiny flowerets and pressed them into a pint measure. Whenever the resulting wine was opened, people in the room began looking for a wandering tomcat! She had used about eight times too much elderflower.

To get the right amount of flowers for elderflower wine, gather them with scissors and snip each flower head through the main stem immediately below the first branchlet of flowers. Put the flower heads in a pint measure and press them down, but not tightly. This gives the right strength of flavour. Then continue the preparation by snipping out and discarding the thickest of the remaining stems.

1pt (600ml) elderflowers
1gal (4.5 litres) water
8oz (230g) sultanas
3½lb (1.6kg) sugar

1 grapefruit
½oz (15g) baker's yeast, or 1 tablet Sauternes yeast

Put the flowers in a pan with water to cover. Bring to the boil, reduce heat at once and simmer for 15 minutes. Chop the sultanas and put with the sugar in mashing tub. Pour the hot liquid through a straining cloth over them and add the rest of the water. Scrub the grapefruit thoroughly and add the thinly peeled rind and the squeezed juice to the mash, discarding the white pith. When lukewarm put in the yeast. Ferment for 3 weeks then strain into fermenting jar with airlock. Taste the wine after 2 months and then at intervals until the right sweetness is achieved, then rack into clean jar, add 1 Campden tablet and store 2–3 months before bottling. Ready for drinking about Christmas of the year it is made. This recipe, using grapefruit instead of 2 lemons, was my own discovery and is my favourite wine. However, the lemons can be used instead of the grapefruit if you prefer.

Garden Champagne
This is made with Golden Drop gooseberries, which must be gathered when very ripe and on a dry day.

1gal (4.5 litres) Golden Drop gooseberries
A handful of raisins
1gal (4.5 litres) water

4lb (1.8kg) sugar
½oz (15g) yeast, champagne yeast if liked

Put the gooseberries in a bucket with the chopped raisins, pour on the water, cover and stand for 14 days stirring and squeezing daily. Strain and squeeze on to the sugar in a fermenting jar, add yeast, ferment 14 days, rack through muslin into clean jar and after 3 days bottle in champagne bottles. Keep 9 months.

Ginger Wine

1½oz (45g) whole ginger
2 lemons, 2 oranges
3lb (1.4kg) sugar

1gal (4.5 litres) water
1lb (450g) raisins
½oz (15g) yeast on slice of toast

Thinly pare the lemons and oranges and put the rind into a pan with the bruised ginger, the sugar and enough of the water to dissolve it. Bring to the boil, simmer for 30 minutes, strain into a bucket and add the remainder of the water, allow to cool.

Chop the raisins and add to the bucket together with the orange and lemon juice and the yeast spread on both sides of the toast. Cover and ferment for 14 days. Strain into jar with airlock, ferment to a finish and bottle. Keep one year.

Gooseberry Wine

4lb (1.8kg) gooseberries picked while green
1gal (4.5 litres) water
3lb (1.4kg) sugar
½oz (15g) yeast

Wash, top and tail the gooseberries and bruise them with a rolling pin or vegetable presser. Put in bucket and add the water, cold. Cover and leave 2 days. Stir in the sugar and stand another 4–5 days, stirring often. Strain into fermenting jar, add yeast, top up if necessary with cold water, ferment to a finish, rack, store and bottle after 8 months. Keep at least one year, but preferably for 2 or 3.

Gorse Wine *(my own recipe)*

2 quarts (2.25 litres) gorse flowers
3lb (1.4kg) white sugar
1 orange
1 lemon
½oz (15g) root ginger
1gal (4.5 litres) cold water
3 tsp dried yeast
Toast

Put in a bucket the gorse flowers, 2lb (900g) of the sugar, the orange and lemon sliced, and the ginger. Pour on the cold water. Cream the yeast with a little sugar and water, spread on a piece of toast and float on top. Cover and ferment for 1 week. Strain on to remaining 1lb (450g) sugar and put in a fermenting jar with airlock. Taste after 6–8 weeks and add a Campden tablet if the wine is dry enough, or else ferment to a finish. Rack, store and bottle as usual. Keep at least 6 months.

Modesty really requires that I should not recommend this recipe as superior to other recipes for Gorse Wine, since it was my own discovery, based on the assumption that yellow colouring and delicate bouquets are best preserved by the use of cold water. But as most people seem to prefer it to others, I will let it be so recorded.

Grapefruit Champagne

7 grapefruit	4lb (1.8kg) sugar
1gal (4.5 litres) cold water	

Cut up the grapefruit in mashing tub. Pour on the water and stand 10 days, covered. Add the sugar by degrees, stirring in well, and stand for a week, stirring daily. Remove scum, strain into fermenting jar. Ferment another 7 days. Strain into champagne bottles, cork well and drink after 3 weeks.

Grape Wine (1) *(using concentrated grape juice)*

A 1kg tin of concentrated grape juice	Wine yeast to make 1gal (4.5 litres) or ½oz (15g) baker's yeast
6pt (3.5 litres) tepid water	10oz (285g) sugar

Dilute the grape juice with the water and put in fermenting jar. Add the yeast and ferment for 10 days. Add 5oz (140g) sugar and ferment for another 5 days. Add remainder of sugar, make up amount to 1gal (4.5 litres) with tepid water and ferment to a finish. Rack the wine and add 1 Campden tablet. When the wine has thrown a firm sediment, bottle off. Keep 3 months before drinking. It is only fair to add that while these wines are drinkable at 3 months, they are quite characterless at that time, and to avoid disappointment I would strongly recommend keeping them in bottles 6 months, when they become quite enjoyable, and if possible 9–12 months, when they become excellent wines.

Grape Wine (2) *(using fresh fruit)*

Grapes	Campden tablets
Sugar	Wine yeast

Take the grapes off the stalks and crush in a large bowl using the hands or a wooden vegetable presser. Strain through muslin, squeezing a little but not wringing too hard. Measure juice and add 1½lb (680g) sugar to each gallon (4.5 litres) stirring well. Now dissolve 2 Campden tablets per gallon (4.5 litres) in a little of the juice and stir in. Cover and leave 24 hours. Then syphon into a fermenting jar and add the yeast. Plug neck of jar with cotton wool, replacing this with an airlock when violent fermentation has died down, which takes 2–3 days. Ferment to a finish. Stand in cool place for 3 weeks, rack and store, bottle off when it has thrown a good sediment. Keep for a year.

Hawthorn Wine: *see* **Mayflower Wine**

Heather Wine

2 quarts (2.25 litres) heather flowers	2 lemons
1gal (4.5 litres) water	2 oranges
3½lb (1.6kg) sugar	1oz (30g) yeast

Boil the heather flowers in the water for an hour. Strain on to the sugar, add the sliced fruit, and then the yeast. Cover and ferment for 14 days. Strain into jar with airlock, ferment to a finish, bottle and keep at least 6 months.

King's Wine
So called in our family because the original recipe was described as 'fit for a king'.

1pt (600ml) (measure) plain boiled rice	4oz (110g) sultanas
1pt (600ml) mashed potato	1gal (4.5 litres) water
3lb (1.4kg) golden syrup	1oz (30g) yeast

This is one of the useful recipes that can be made from leftovers; leftover boiled rice or rice pudding will do, and leftover potato if it has not been too heavily salted. A little pepper does no harm if it happens to be already in the potato. However, you can start from scratch by boiling 5oz (140g) rice in a pint (600ml) of boiling water with just a pinch of salt, until the water is absorbed. Scrub the potatoes well but don't peel, cut in half and boil until soft but not squashy, and mash. About half a dozen

medium sized potatoes will be needed. Mix together with the rice, syrup and chopped sultanas. Add the cold water and then the yeast. Cover well and stir daily for 12 days. At about this stage the wine, at first very milky, will begin to clear slightly. Strain into fermenting jar and fit airlock. When it throws a sediment, rack into a clean jar, ferment to a finish and bottle. Keep at least 6 months. However, like all wines with starchy ingredients, it is only tolerable at that age. Kept for 3 years, with several rackings in the earlier stages, it finishes as a magnificent dry wine of sherry type and strength.

Lemon Wine

10 lemons	4lb (1.8kg) granulated sugar
1gal (4.5 litres) water	½oz (15g) yeast on toast

Wash the lemons carefully. Put the thinly peeled rind of 5 of the lemons into a bucket. Dissolve the sugar in the water and bring to the boil. Boil for 30 minutes, skimming if required. Pour it boiling over the rinds, cover and leave until cool. Then add the juice of all the lemons and float the toast spread with the yeast on top. Cover well and ferment for 2–3 days. Strain into a jar with an airlock and ferment to a finish. Then rack into a fresh jar, add 2–3fl oz (60–90ml) of brandy if liked, and store for 4 months before bottling. Keep at least another 6 months in bottle before use.

Lime Blossom Wine

Pull lime blossoms on the spray from the tree when fully open and let them dry a few hours in the sun. Dried and stored blossoms can also be used.

1pt (600ml) lime blossoms (½pt [300ml] if fully dried). Pack the measure but do not press down hard.	3½lb (1.6kg) sugar
	8oz (230g) raisins
	1 wineglass of cold tea
	1oz (30g) yeast on large slice of toast
1gal (4.5 litres) water	

Put the flowers in a pan with the water and simmer for 15 minutes. Put into a jar and add the sugar, raisins, cold tea and yeast on toast (spread both sides). Ferment for 14 days. Strain into a fermenting jar and rack as soon as it throws a sediment. Store and bottle as usual. Keep for 9 months. Don't omit the preliminary wilting of the flowers in sunshine as this brings out the flavour.

Mangold Wine *(mangelwurzel)*

4lb (1.8kg) mangolds	1gal (4.5 litres) water
2 lemons	3½lb (1.6kg) sugar
1 orange	1oz (30g) baker's yeast

Scrub the mangolds and slice them into a large saucepan. Add the thinly peeled rinds of the fruit and cover well with water. Boil until mangolds are just tender. Strain on to the sugar, stir well, add rest of water and fruit juices. When cool add yeast and leave, covered, for 24 hours. Strain into fermentation jar and cover or fit airlock. Ferment to a finish, rack, store and bottle. Keep for a year or until it clears.

Marigold Wine

2 quarts (2.25 litres) marigold flowers (no stalks)	2 oranges
	1 lemon
3lb (1.4kg) sugar	1oz (30g) yeast
1gal (4.5 litres) water	

Dissolve the sugar in the water and bring to the boil. Put the flowers and thinly peeled rinds and juice of the fruit in mashing tub. Pour on the hot syrup. When cool add yeast. Cover and ferment for a week. Strain into fermenting jar, ferment to a finish, move to a cool place for 3 weeks then rack, store and bottle. Keep 6 months.

Marrow Wine

5lb (2.2kg) marrow (trimmings and seeds from jam-making can be used)
2 lemons
2 oranges
1oz (30g) root ginger
1gal (4.5 litres) water
3lb (1.4kg) sugar
½oz (15g) yeast

Grate or finely chop the marrow, slice the lemons and oranges and well bruise the ginger, put all in a bucket, pour over the boiling water and stand, well covered, for 10 days, stirring daily. Strain on to the sugar in fermenting jar, mix well, add yeast, ferment for 7 days and then rack into clean jar, ferment to a finish, store and bottle as usual. Keep for 6 months.

Mayflower Wine (Hawthorn)

2 quarts (2.25 litres) mayblossom
1gal (4.5 litres) water
3lb (1.4kg) sugar
1lb (450g) wheat
8oz (230g) raisins
1oz (30g) yeast on toast

Boil the sugar and water together, pour over the mayblossom in a bucket and allow to cool. Then add chopped raisins, wheat and yeast on toast. Ferment for 16 days, stirring daily. Strain into jar with airlock, allow to finish, and bottle as usual. Said to be a very strong wine. Keep 9 months to a year.

Mrs Sinkins Wine

Good wine can be made from pinks and carnations, and the best kind is made with the famous old mop-headed white pink, 'Mrs Sinkins'. This is often found in profusion in old gardens so it should not be too difficult to get the required ½gal (2.5 litres) of flower heads. Another good one is the so-called 'Pink Mrs Sinkins', correctly called 'Excelsior'.

2 quarts (2.25 litres) heads of pinks
1gal (4.5 litres) water
3lb (1.4kg) sugar

8oz (230g) raisins
1 orange
1 lemon
1oz (30g) yeast spread on toast

Put the flower heads in a bucket, bring the water to the boil and pour it over them, and leave well covered for 3 days, stirring daily. Strain and squeeze on to the sugar and chopped raisins, add the fruit sliced, and float the toast with yeast on top. Ferment for 3 weeks, strain into jar with airlock, ferment to a finish or add a Campden tablet before the wine gets too dry, rack, store, and bottle after a month or so. Keep 6 months.

Mulberry Wine

2 quarts (2.25 litres) mulberries
1gal (4.5 litres) water

3½lb (1.6kg) white sugar
1oz (30g) yeast on toast

Boil the mulberries in the water for 30 minutes, then strain on to the sugar. Leave till cool, float the yeast on toast on the top, cover and ferment for 14 days, skim and strain into fermenting jar, finish and bottle as usual. Keep at least a year.

Orange Wine

5 large oranges, 1 Seville orange
1 lemon
1gal (4.5 litres) water
3lb (1.4kg) white sugar

1lb (450g) wheat or 3 cakes Shredded Wheat
4oz (110g) raisins
1oz (30g) yeast

Peel the coloured part of the fruit rinds thinly and boil in the water for 15 minutes. Strain on to the sugar, wheat and raisins and add the squeezed fruit juice. When lukewarm add yeast. Cover well, ferment for 21 days, strain into jar with airlock, ferment to a finish and bottle. Keep 9 months.

Orchard Wine
Excellent for using up windfalls.

4lb (1.8kg) apples
4lb (1.8kg) pears
1gal (4.5 litres) water

3½lb (1.6kg) sugar
8oz (230g) raisins

Wash and cut up the fruit, put in a bucket, add water, sugar and chopped raisins, cover well and ferment for a month, squeezing and stirring daily. Strain into jar with airlock, ferment to a finish and store and bottle as usual. Keep 9–12 months.

Parsley Wine

1lb (450g) parsley (freshly gathered)	2 oranges
	2 lemons
1gal (4.5 litres) water	4lb (1.8kg) sugar
1oz (30g) root ginger	½oz (15g) yeast on toast

Put the parsley into 1gal (4.5 litres) boiling water and let it stand, covered, for 24 hours. Strain out the parsley and boil the liquor for 20 minutes, with the ginger and the thinly peeled rind of the oranges and lemons. Pour on to the sugar and add the fruit juices. When lukewarm float in the yeast on toast. Cover and ferment for 4 days. Strain into fermenting jar, fit airlock and ferment to a finish. Rack, store and bottle as usual. Keep at least 6 months, the longer the better.

Parsnip Wine

4lb (1.8kg) parsnips	½oz (15g) root ginger (optional)
2 lemons	3lb (1.4kg) sugar
1 orange	¾oz (22g) baker's yeast or a
1gal (4.5 litres) water	Sherry or Burgundy yeast

Scrub the parsnips well but do not peel them, cut into slices ½in (12mm) thick. Boil the parsnips and thinly peeled rinds of the fruit in the water, adding ginger if liked. Do not overboil as this causes cloudiness in the wine; the parsnips must be only just tender. Strain on to the sugar and stir well. When lukewarm add fruit juices and yeast. Cover well and leave for 24 hours in a warm place, then pour into fermenting jar with airlock and leave to ferment to a finish (about 14 days). Remove to a cooler place and after 1 or 2 weeks syphon into a clean jar. Cork or put in airlock and leave 6 months. Bottle and keep at least another 6 months, but the longer the better.

Peach Wine

Not exactly in the economy class, but even if the peaches and the white wine both have to be bought the cost is little more than half that of a cheap wine from the wine shop. If you or your friends have a peach tree and can use windfalls and home-made grape wine, it costs next to nothing!

4lb (1.8kg) peaches	A bottle of sweet white grape wine
1gal (4.5 litres) water	
2½lb (1.1kg) loaf or preserving sugar	1oz (30g) gum arabic
	1oz (30g) powdered chalk
1oz (30g) baker's yeast on toast	

Use filtered rainwater for this wine if possible, and slightly underripe fruit. Slice the peaches into the water, keeping back the stones. Add the sugar, bring to the boil and skim until the liquid looks clear. Crack the peach stones and put the kernels in a large crock. Pour on the hot liquid. When lukewarm spread the yeast on toast and float on top. Cover and ferment for 2 weeks. Add the bottle of wine and strain into a jar with airlock. Leave it for 6 months, checking airlock regularly. Now take a little of the wine, warm it slightly and dissolve in it the gum arabic and the chalk (bought as precipitated chalk or powdered calcium carbonate). Return this mixture to the fermenting jar, taking great care throughout not to disturb the lees. Bottle the wine after 1 week and leave for a further 8 months before drinking.

Pink Wine *(garden pinks): see* **Mrs Sinkins**

Pea Pod Wine

This is another wine like bramble tip, that gathers flavour and strength with keeping. As much as 2, 3 or even 8 years have been mentioned by various authorities, but some say it is good at 6 months.

2gal (9 litres) pea pods	4lb (1.8kg) sugar
1gal (4.5 litres) water	½oz (15g) yeast on toast

Boil the pods in the water until they have turned yellow, then strain on to the sugar. When cool add yeast and ferment for 21 days, then skim or strain into a jar fitted with an airlock, ferment to a finish, rack and store until the wine clears before bottling.

Pomona Wine (Cider Wine)

This is made from cider, which should be good and fresh to achieve the best results.

1gal (4.5 litres) cider	¼pt (150ml) brandy
2lb (900g) sugar	

Dissolve the sugar in the cider, put in a jar with airlock, and leave for 3 days. Then add the brandy, cork the jar, and store for 9 months before bottling.

Potato Hock

6 medium size raw potatoes	4lb (1.8kg) sugar
1lb (450g) raisins	1gal (4.5 litres) warm water
2 oranges	½oz (15g) yeast
3 lemons	

Chop the raisins and slice the oranges and lemons. Clean but do not peel potatoes, and cut in ½in (12mm) cubes. Mix in the sugar and warm water and when cool add the yeast. Cover and stand for 2 weeks. Skim, strain and put in a fermenting jar to ferment to a finish. Rack, store and bottle as usual. Keep 9 months.

Potato Wine

To use up small potatoes. This is a 'no yeast' recipe, but a suitable white wine yeast could be used.

½gal (2.25 litres) small potatoes   3lb (1.4kg) granulated sugar
1gal (4.5 litres) water   2 oranges
1oz (30g) root ginger   2 lemons

Wash the potatoes well and cut them in half, put into the cold water with the ginger, bring to the boil and boil for 10 minutes. Strain the hot liquid on to the sugar and sliced fruit. Cover and stand while it ferments for a fortnight. Strain into fermenting jar, ferment to a finish, rack, store and bottle after 3 months. Keep 6 months or longer.

Primrose Wine

If ever it is possible to gather so many primrose flowers, this is a justly famous wine!

3 quarts (3.5 litres) primrose   2 lemons
  heads   3½lb (1.6kg) sugar
1gal (4.5 litres) boiling water   ½oz (15g) yeast
2 oranges

Pour the boiling water over the flowers and sliced fruit. Stand for 5 days, stirring daily, then strain on to sugar in fermenting jar, add yeast, ferment 14 days and then rack through muslin into clean jar, ferment to a finish, rack, store and bottle after 1 month. Keep at least 6 months.

Prune Sherry

2lb (900g) prunes   8oz (230g) raisins
1gal (4.5 litres) water   1oz (30g) yeast on large slice toast
4lb (1.8kg) sugar

Cover the prunes with the cold water and stand, covered, for 14 days. Stir and squeeze daily, then strain and squeeze on to sugar and chopped raisins. Float the toast with yeast on top, ferment for 21 days, skim and strain into jar with airlock, ferment to a finish, rack, store and bottle after 2–3 months. Keep at least a year.

Quince Wine

20 large ripe quinces or japonica fruit
1gal (4.5 litres) water
2lb (900g) preserving sugar
2 lemons
½oz (15g) yeast on toast

Wash the quinces and grate them into a preserving pan, discarding the cores. Pour on the water, bring to the boil and simmer 15 minutes, strain and squeeze through muslin into a bucket, add the sugar, thinly peeled rind and juice of lemons, and stir well. When cool add the yeast spread on the toast, cover and leave for 24 hours. Then strain into fermenting jar, make up to 1gal (4.5 litres) with cold boiled water if necessary, fit airlock and ferment to a finish. Rack, store and bottle as usual and keep as long as possible as it goes on improving.

Raisin Wine

2lb (900g) large raisins
3½lb (1.6kg) sugar
1lb (450g) wheat
4 lemons
1gal (4.5 litres) boiling water
1oz (30g) tea (dry weight)
1oz (30g) yeast

Chop the raisins and put in a bucket with the sugar, wheat and sliced lemons. Pour on the water and stir well. Make the tea into a strong brew, using a small teapot, and strain into the mixture. When cool add yeast and ferment for 21 days, stirring daily. Strain into a jar, ferment to a finish, rack, store and bottle as usual and keep for a year.

Raisin and Elderberry Wine

6lb (2.75kg) raisins
1gal (4.5 litres) water
1 quart (1.2 litres) elderberry juice
1oz (30g) yeast spread on toast

Shred or chop the raisins, put in a bucket and pour the water boiling hot, over them. Cover and leave to stand for 9–10 days, stirring daily or more frequently if possible.

Gather elderberries fully ripe, strip them off the stalks, put in a stoneware jar and stand this in a pan of boiling water or in a slow oven for several hours to extract the juice (overnight in a range oven, if you have one, with a lid on the jar, of course). Strain through muslin, squeezing to get the most juice, and add to the raisins (proportions as above). Add the yeast on toast. Cover and ferment for 3 days, strain into a jar with airlock, ferment to a finish, rack into storage jar and keep 9 months before bottling. Keep at least another 9 months in bottle. This is very like port, and at the time of writing would work out at approximately 20 per cent of the cost.

Rhubarb Champagne
When I lived in Yorkshire in the 1930s there were in south Yorkshire vast areas of rhubarb fields, and I was told that before the introduction of the *appelation* rules in France (and perhaps also after) this rhubarb was exported thither in great quantities to be used in 'champagne'. Possibly vine prunings were used with it too.

1gal (4.5 litres) rhubarb	4lb (1.8kg) white sugar
20 vine leaves with stems	1gal (4.5 litres) cold water

Cut up the rhubarb very small and mix the vine leaves with it. Add the sugar and water; stir until sugar is dissolved. Let it ferment 14 days, strain into clean jar, ferment 3 days, then bottle in champagne or beer bottles, and keep in safe storage where a burst bottle might do no harm, eg in strong wooden crates in an outhouse or shed. Alternatively, cork lightly and check frequently for blown corks. Keep at least 6 months.

Rice Pudding Wine: *see* King's Wine

Rice Wine
The recipe for rice wine is said to be the nearest European equivalent to sake but is possibly more like a mixture of sake and mirin (Japanese sweet wine).

Suitable for Japanese cookery recipes such as Japanese Cold Chicken (p121).

3lb (1.4kg) rice	1gal (4.5 litres) water
3lb (1.4kg) sugar	1oz (30g) yeast
1lb (450g) large raisins	

Put rice, sugar and chopped raisins into bucket and cover with warm water. When lukewarm add the activated yeast. Stir often for the first 3 days and then leave fermenting for a week. Strain into fermenting jar, ferment to a finish, store 3 months before bottling and do not drink before the wine is a year old.

Romany Claret

2lb (900g) beetroot	3lb (1.4kg) sugar
1gal (4.5 litres) water	12oz (350g) apples
1½lb (680g) potatoes	½oz (15g) baker's yeast

Wash and cut up the beetroot, working as quickly as possible over the pan of water. Bring to the boil, boil for 20 minutes and remove from heat. Scrub the potatoes very thoroughly and cut in ½in (12mm) cubes; put them in the bucket or crock with the sugar and pour the warm beetroot and liquid over them. Mix well, stand for 14 days well covered. Strain the liquid into a wide-necked jar with the apples cut up small and the yeast. Ferment for 7 days and then rack and strain into fermentation jar, fit airlock and ferment to a finish. When it throws a firm sediment, rack, store for 3 months, then bottle. Keep at least 6 months. A strong red wine maturing to tawny, of excellent flavour.

Root Wine

1lb (450g) each of carrot trimmings, turnip peelings, potato peelings and parsnip trimmings	2 lemons
	2 oranges
Water	½oz (15g) root ginger
3½lb (1.6kg) sugar (half brown and half white)	½oz (15g) baker's yeast

As the vegetable trimmings are collected, put them in a saucepan, cover with water, bring to the boil and simmer until tender. Then strain and squeeze through a muslin cloth, and keep the liquid in a covered jar until you have 1gal (4.5 litres). Take some of the liquid, dissolve the sugar, and add to the jar. Peel lemons and oranges thinly and put in the peel and juice. Finally add the ginger and the activated yeast and stand the jar in a warm place.

Ferment for 3 weeks, rack into a clean fermentation jar, ferment to a finish. Rack again, store for 3 months, bottle and keep at least 6 months.

Rose Hip Wine

This recipe was originally devised to use rose hip pulp left over from making syrup, but could be adapted to use whole rose hips.

3½lb (1.6kg) rose hip pulp (or 3lb [1.4kg] fresh hips crushed and boiled for 10 minutes)
1lb (450g) mixed chopped carrot and turnip
4oz (110g) sultanas
Peel of 1 orange

1 tbsp lemon juice
2 tbsp strong tea
1gal (4.5 litres) cold water
3lb (1.4kg) sugar
3 tsp dried yeast
1 rye biscuit

Boil the carrot and turnip mixture until soft. Put the rose hip pulp, vegetables, sultanas, fruit peel, lemon juice and tea into a bucket, add the water and stir in 2lb (900g) of the sugar. Cream the yeast with some of the liquid, spread it on the rye biscuit and float it on top. Cover and ferment for a week, stirring and squeezing daily. Add remaining 1lb (500g) sugar and ferment for another week. Strain into jar with airlock, ferment to a finish, rack, store and bottle as usual. Keep for 9 months to a year before use.

Sack, or Saragossa Wine

1gal (4.5 litres) water
A handful of fennel roots

2 or 3 sprigs of rue
3lb (1.4kg) honey

Boil the rue and fennel roots in all or some of the water for half an hour. Strain, and add the honey, boil the mixture again for 2 hours, skimming as necessary. Allow to cool, put in a fermenting jar with airlock, making up amount if necessary to 1¼gal (5.7 litres), and store carefully for a year. Then bottle and keep at least 3 months before drinking.

As with all honey recipes, this is mainly for the beekeepers nowadays, but the rue need not pose too much of a problem as so many gardens now have the ornamental form *Ruta graveolens* 'Jackman's Blue'.

Sage Wine

2 quarts (2.25 litres) fresh sage
  leaves
4lb (1.8kg) raisins

1gal (4.5 litres) water
½oz (15g) yeast

Chop the raisins and sage roughly and put in mashing tub or bucket. Boil the water, leave until lukewarm, and then pour over the fruits and leaves and add the yeast. Stir well and leave covered for 5–6 days, stirring daily. Strain and squeeze into fermenting jar. Let it ferment to a finish, rack into clean jar, add ¼pt (150ml) brandy (optional) and store for 6 months. Bottle and keep for a month; it can then be drunk, but is better for keeping longer. Said to be a good tonic.

Sake: *see* Rice Wine

Tomato Wine

8lb (3.6kg) ripe tomatoes
½oz (15g) root ginger
3½lb (1.6kg) sugar

1gal (4.5 litres) water
1 tbsp salt
1oz (30g) baker's yeast on toast

Bruise the ginger and boil it with the sugar and water for 20 minutes. Turn it boiling on to the tomatoes and salt. When lukewarm add the yeast spread on both sides of the toast, float in the liquid and leave to ferment 21 days, squeezing the tomatoes daily. Strain into a fermenting jar. Ferment to a finish, rack and bottle. This is a good tonic. Keep 6 months before use.

Turnip Wine

6lb (2.75kg) turnips
1gal (4.5 litres) water
2 oranges
2 lemons
3½lb (1.6kg) sugar

½oz (15g) root ginger (optional)
1lb (450g) wheat or 2–3 cakes of
  Shredded Wheat
2oz (60g) chopped raisins
1oz (30g) yeast

Scrub, cut up and simmer the turnips in the water until tender. Wash and slice the lemons and oranges and put in a bucket with the sugar. Add the ginger, bruised, if required. Strain the hot liquid over them, allow to stand until lukewarm, add the wheat, raisins and yeast, cover and ferment for 15 days. Strain into jar with airlock, ferment to a finish, and bottle. Keep for one year.

Tutti-Frutti Wine

4oz (110g) sultanas, chopped
8 orange skins
6 banana skins
1lb (450g) apple cores and peelings, or windfalls
1lb (450kg) blackberries or other soft fruit
3lb (1.4kg) white sugar
Rind and juice of 2 lemons
½oz (15g) baker's yeast or 1 tablet Sauternes yeast
Cooked beetroot

Prepare the fruit contents as they become available. Put the chopped sultanas in a bucket or jar, add the banana skins, apple cores, etc as you go along, keeping just covered with cold water. Boil the blackberries in water to cover for 10 minutes and add to the mash. Stir well daily but be careful not to squeeze the orange peel. When all the fruit waste is in (this may take a fortnight or even more) keep another 3–4 days stirring daily, then strain and measure the liquid and make up to 1gal (4.5 litres) with cold water. Put in a fermenting jar and add sugar, lemon rind and juice, and yeast. Keep an eye on the colour, which should be a delicate rose, and if it should be too pale, add 2 or 3 slices of chopped cooked beetroot. After three weeks, rack and strain into clean jar, ferment to a finish, rack, store and bottle. Keep at least 6 months.

Vine Leaf Wine

If you can get hold of prunings from vines, the young fresh leaves and stems are full of flavour.

5lb (2.25kg) vine leaves and stems   3½lb (1.6kg) sugar
1gal (4.5 litres) boiling water

Put the leaves in a bucket and pour on the boiling water. Cover and stand for 3 days, then strain and squeeze on to the sugar. Stir until dissolved. Ferment for 10 days. Skim and strain into clean jar, ferment to a finish, rack, strain and bottle. Keep 6 months.

White Currant Wine or English Champagne

3pt (1.8 litres) white currants   ½oz (15g) yeast
1gal (4.5 litres) water   ¼oz (7g) isinglass
3lb (1.4kg) white sugar

Boil the water and sugar together for 30 minutes, skimming as necessary. String the currants into a bucket, pour on the boiling liquid, cover and leave until lukewarm. Add the yeast, ferment for 2 days, then strain through muslin into fermenting jar with airlock. Ferment to a finish, rack, add isinglass and store for a month. Now bottle in strong bottles, adding a small lump of candy sugar or preserving sugar to each bottle. Cork well and store carefully. Keep at least 6 months.

Whortleberry Wine (Bilberry, Blaeberry)

Whortleberries   Water
Granulated sugar

Measure the berries and allow 1gal (4.5 litres) water to 1gal (4.5 litres) fruit. Put the fruit into a bucket and pour over it the water, boiling. Cover and stand overnight. Strain and squeeze out all the juice. Measure again and allow 2lb (900g) sugar to each gallon (4.5 litres) of juice. Stir in the sugar, put in fermenting jar, ferment to a finish, rack and store for 9 months before bottling, and at least another 6 months in bottles.

These are all the ingredients needed, but a few cloves and a piece of cinnamon, or a few leaves of lavender or rosemary may be added. Yeast may be used for the fermentation if preferred.

3

MEAD, BEER, CIDER, COOKING WINES AND VINEGAR

MEAD AND METHEGLIN

Mead and metheglin were once the drinks of the people, but have become progressively less so as sugar has replaced honey in our diet. In addition, the price of honey makes these drinks comparatively very expensive. However, the price at the time of writing works out at about the same as that of wines made with commercial concentrated grape juice. Mead, correctly, is made from the fermentation of honey and water with no other addition than yeast. Where herbs and spices are added the result is not mead but metheglin. Some commercial so-called meads are made from raisin wine flavoured with honey and are very sickly. A true mead, especially dry mead, is not unlike amontillado and not sickly at all.

Modern honey is highly purified and, if used to make mead or metheglin, may give a poor fermentation as a result. Consequently the yeast should be activated with the addition of either special mead nutrients, or the following home-made mixture:

For fermenting 1gal of mead

¼pt (150ml) water
1 level tbsp sugar
¼ level tsp tartaric acid

¼ level tsp Marmite
¼ level tsp ammonium phosphate
  or 1 yeast nutrient tablet

Begin 2 days ahead of mead-making. Boil the water, sugar, tartaric acid and Marmite. Cover and set aside until just cool enough to put in a bottle; cork the bottle. When the mixture is at blood heat add the ammonium phosphate or yeast nutrient tablet and shake until dissolved. Activate the yeast in another bottle using a small amount of this liquid. When well frothed (about 48 hours) add the rest of the nutrient and pour all into the mead when it is at blood heat.

Dry Mead

3lb (1.4kg) honey (if liquid
  honey, 3½lb [1.6kg])
½oz (15g) baker's yeast or mead
  yeast, prepared as above

Water to make up to 1gal (4.5 litres)

Mix the honey and water well in a bucket previously marked at 1gal (4.5 litres) level. Pour into a large pan (or smaller pan in 2 or 3 batches if necessary). Bring to the boil, simmer 5 minutes, and set aside to cool. Strain into fermenting jar; when at blood heat add the prepared yeast, ferment to a finish, rack and bottle. This will keep indefinitely, and in fact improves with age.

Sweet Mead

4lb (1.8kg) honey (if liquid, 4½lb
  [2kg])
Water to make 1gal (4.5 litres)

½oz (15g) baker's yeast or mead yeast

Proceed exactly in the same way as for dry mead. If it ferments out and becomes too dry, warm 4oz (110g) honey by standing the jar in hot water, mix well with some of the mead, return the mixture to fermenting jar and leave for 3 weeks before racking.

Metheglin

5lb (2.25kg) honey
1gal (4.5 litres) water
1 lemon
A sprig of rosemary

A sprig of balm
½oz (15g) root ginger (optional)
¾oz (22g) baker's yeast or mead
yeast

Peel the lemon thinly and simmer in the water together with the herbs and ginger for 20 minutes. Strain on to the honey and mix well. When lukewarm, add the lemon juice and yeast. Cover and leave for 24 hours. Put in jar with airlock, ferment to a finish, rack, store and bottle.

The flavouring can be varied by using an orange instead of a lemon, rue, hops or sweetbriar in place of rosemary, and cloves or cinnamon in place of ginger. Ground ivy or 'alehoof' was an old-time flavouring used in place of hops, and this or other herbs of which you like the flavour may also be tried.

Sack: *see* Chapter 2

BEER

The days are long gone when every household of any size brewed its own beer, and very large establishments even had their own malting floor. Commercial beermaking kits for the amateur are convenient and not unduly expensive, but it is not a bad thing to know a basic beermaking recipe, and I therefore give it in its original form and quantities.

To make 12gal (54 litres) of malt beer

1 bushel (36 litres) pale malt
15gal (68 litres) water
8oz (230g) hops

2lb (900g) moist sugar (light brown today)
½pt (300ml) fresh yeast

Put the water in a large copper and bring it to the boil. Bale out about ⅔ of this water into a mash-tub with a bung-hole, placing a huckmuck or strainer inside the tub at the bung-hole. Cool for about 20 minutes and then carefully stir in the malt so that there are no lumps. Cover and let it stand for 2 hours. Drain off the liquid from above the malt into another tub, add the remaining

⅓ of the boiling water to the malt, soak again, then draw off and put back together with the first liquid into the copper, add the hops and boil together for 2 hours. Put the sugar into a tub and strain the hot liquid over it. Leave until lukewarm and then add the yeast. Cover and leave until next day, skim off the yeast and pour the beer into casks or jars. Let it ferment for about a week, keeping topped up with spare beer. Close down, but not too tightly.

Other beer recipes are given in the section on 'Summer Drinks' in Chapter 5.

CIDER

The first thing to say about cider is that it should not be made at home for drinking. Rough cider is near-poisonous, can produce racking headaches and sickness, and is not for the home brewer.

A kind of half-cider, half-apple wine can be made, however, which is perfectly all right for use in cooking.

Cooking Cider

Windfall apples, small ones are Water
best Sugar

Wash the apples, cut them up and place in a deep earthenware jar. Pour on cold water to cover, protect the top of the jar with fourfold cotton cloth and let the apples stand for 10 days, stirring daily. When fermentation dies down, strain and measure the liquid. Stir in 1¼lb (550g) sugar to each gallon (4.5 litres), and if liked add a piece of beetroot to improve the colour. When sugar is thoroughly dissolved cover again for 24 hours, then bottle it but put a cottonwool plug in the bottles instead of corks. After about 14 days, when it has ceased working, cork well but do not use screw stoppers and store where an occasional popped cork will not matter. Use after 2–3 months.

Small quantities made in succession are best, to avoid over-long keeping, but if it does go vinegary it is still, of course, usable in savoury dishes.

COOKING WINES

In my opinion at any rate, Marrow Rum, Rhubarb Brandy, and Carrot Whisky are better for cooking than for drinking, although there is no accounting for tastes, and certainly for those who like sweet drinks, Marrow Rum can be enjoyed as a liqueur once it is two years old or over. It mustn't be forgotten that rum, brandy and whisky are distilled spirits, whereas their vegetable namesakes are fermented liquors. The latter therefore can't be used where spirit is required as a preservative, but are perfectly all right where it is a flavouring that is required—for instance in cakes, puddings, desserts, soups and stews. The old, true and Pickwickian milk punch must be made with genuine rum, but Dutch Punch for example would be a good warming drink made with Marrow Rum, and you might even try a Tom and Jerry made with Marrow Rum and Rhubarb Brandy, remembering that less sugar would be required owing to their sweetness.

Perhaps the most useful of cooking wines is the equivalent of a red *vin ordinaire* for such dishes as Coq au Vin, and it is well worth using a claret made from concentrated grape juice for this purpose. However, red country or garden wines are the next best thing.

The traditional method of making Marrow Rum by hanging up the marrow and using it as its own fermenting jar is great fun, but a bit chancy and not strictly necessary. It is given for the benefit of those with the available space and the spirit of adventure, but the second recipe is equally good and safer.

Marrow Rum (1)

1 large vegetable marrow	½oz (15g) baker's yeast
Demerara sugar	1 orange or 2 tbsp orange juice

Choose a well-ripened marrow with a tough, hard skin. Using a bread saw, cut the stalk end off about 2in (5cm) from the end and scoop out the pith and seeds. Pack the cavity with Demerara sugar. Mix ½oz (15g) yeast with 2 tbsp lukewarm water and the juice of the orange. Pour over the sugar in the marrow. Replace the cut-off piece and seal well with adhesive tape. Suspend the marrow, cut end uppermost, in a muslin bag in a warm place. A basin beneath will prevent possible mess from leakage. Inspect at intervals, and when the liquid shows signs of leaking out (about 3 weeks) make a hole in the bottom of the marrow and allow the liquid to run through a funnel into a clean jar and fit airlock. Ferment to a finish. Bottle and keep as long as possible—the older it is the better it becomes.

Marrow Rum (2)

1 ripe marrow	½oz (15g) baker's yeast or 1 tsp
Demerara sugar	dried yeast
2 tbsp orange juice	A little lukewarm water

Wash the marrow and cut into 1in (2.5cm) cubes, discarding the seeds and pith. Weigh the marrow cubes and take three quarters of their weight of Demerara sugar. Using glass confectionery jars or similar vessels, put the marrow and sugar in alternate layers until jars are filled. A large marrow yields about 6lb (2.75kg) of cubes, which, together with the sugar, will fill 1gal (4.5 litres) measure approx. On first filling the jars should be of a size that does not use all the marrow; reserve about a quarter of it for topping up. Now pour on the orange juice and leave, well covered, for about an hour when the sugar will have liquidised and the marrow sunk in the jars. Add remaining marrow, leaving an air space at the top for fermentation. Mix the yeast with about a teacup of lukewarm water and pour in. Cover well and ferment for about 3 weeks, stirring and pressing every 2–3 days. Then strain into clean jar with airlock, ferment to a finish and bottle as for Marrow Rum (1).

Rhubarb Brandy

6lb (2.75kg) rhubarb	2lb (900g) brown sugar
8oz (230g) raw potato	2 quarts (2.25 litres) boiling
8oz (230g) raisins	water
8oz (230g) pearl barley	1oz (30g) baker's yeast

Wash the rhubarb and potatoes and cut them up small. Chop the raisins. Put the rhubarb, potatoes, raisins, barley and sugar into a bucket or jar. Pour on the boiling water. When at blood heat add the yeast. Cover and ferment for 3 weeks. Strain into a fresh jar, cover and leave till fermentation ceases, bottle and keep for 6 months. Use in cakes, puddings, brandysnaps, etc.

Carrot Whisky

6lb (2.75kg) carrots	4lb (1.8kg) sugar
1gal (4.5 litres) water	12oz (350g) chopped raisins
2 lemons	1lb (450g) wheat
2 oranges	1oz (30g) baker's yeast

Wash carrots well, cut up and boil until tender using the 1gal (4.5 litres) of water. Wash and slice the lemons and oranges. Strain the hot carrot liquid on to them. Add the sugar and stir until dissolved. When cool, add the raisins and wheat and put in the yeast. Cover well, ferment for a fortnight, strain into a fermenting jar and ferment to a finish. Rack and bottle as usual. Keep at least 6 months.

VINEGARS

The following recipes are for culinary vinegars, not to be confused with raspberry vinegar and similar recipes which are in the nature of cordials for treating coughs and colds.

Apple Vinegar

1gal (4.5 litres) sour apples (or apple trimmings)

Water
Malt vinegar

Bruise the apples well and put them in a bucket. When they start to ferment add water barely to cover the fruit, and keep it topped up. At the end of a month strain and measure the liquid. To each gallon (4.5 litres) add ½pt (300ml) vinegar that has been previously boiled and reduced from 1pt (600ml). Bottle and use after 6 weeks.

Fruit Vinegars

Using a red fruit such as blackberries or plums, take 1gal (4.5 litres) fruit to 1gal (4.5 litres) water, add 1½lb (680g) sugar and ½oz (15g) yeast and ferment uncovered. Strain, bottle and keep 3 months.

Any of these vinegars can be used as a basis for the following flavoured vinegars, which are useful for cooking purposes, making fresh relishes to serve with cold meat or curry, or as non-fattening salad dressings, etc.

Tarragon Vinegar

Put 2 handfuls tarragon leaves into a cider bottle or a large wine bottle. Fill up the bottle with wine vinegar, leave corked for 3 weeks, then strain and bottle.

Mint Vinegar

Proceed as for tarragon vinegar but use 4 handfuls of mint leaves.

Garlic Vinegar

1 bulb garlic   2pt (1.2 litres) vinegar

Split up the garlic bulb into cloves, put in a basin, boil the vinegar and pour on to the garlic, cover and leave for 24 hours, then strain into bottles.

Chilli Vinegar

Steep 1oz (30g) chillies in 1pt (600ml) vinegar with a pinch of salt. Leave for 10 days (use screw-topped jars or large bottles). Shake daily. Strain into bottles.

Economy Vinegars

As well as using waste fruit for vinegar, lees from winemaking may be strained and racked two or three times in open jars to make vinegar. Vinegary or otherwise poor wine may be allowed to vinegarise further in an open jar and makes very good vinegar.

4

LIQUEURS AND SUNDRIES

LIQUEURS

Among the most expensive of all luxury goods are liqueurs, fruit-flavoured brandies, and *bonnes bouches* generally, but a good deal of money can be saved by making them at home. In many cases the constituent which makes these cost so much is the time taken in their preparation; but even where expensive ingredients such as brandy are required, they can be made for about half the retail price, at home.

Let's begin with something that makes many people sigh ecstatically.

Cherry Brandy

6lb (2.75kg) Morello cherries   6pt (3.5 litres) brandy
1½lb (680g) crystal candy sugar

Mix the cherries and sugar, put in a crock and pour the brandy over (the crock should be almost filled). Cover and leave for 6 months. Strain, bottle immediately and cork well. Keeps indefinitely and goes on improving. One sixth of this recipe, made with a bottle of 'duty-free from the airport', is probably nearer the mark for most of us! The cherries can be eaten by the hard-headed.

Blackcurrant Brandy

2lb (900g) blackcurrants
1oz (30g) ground ginger
2pt (1 litre) brandy

1lb (450g) loaf sugar
¼pt (150ml) water

String and crush the blackcurrants using a wooden spoon, stir in the ginger and pour on the brandy. Cover closely and leave for 2–3 days. Dissolve the sugar in the water. Strain the brandy mixture into it, stir well, strain again and bottle in small bottles, sealing well.

Advocaat

6 fresh eggs
3 lemons

4oz (110g) brown sugar
½pt (300ml) brandy

Wipe the eggs and place in a wide-necked glass jar with a stopper. Squeeze off the lemon juice and pour over the eggs. Stopper the jar and leave it to stand for a week. At the end of this time the eggs will have completely dissolved. Add the sugar and whisk all well together. Strain, pour on the brandy, and bottle. Allow it to stand for a month before use.

Said to be an excellent pick-me-up for convalescents.

Athol Brose

1 gill (150ml) oatmeal cream (see below) 2oz (60g) fluid honey
Whisky

Mix some oatmeal with sufficient water to make a thickish paste, leave for an hour, then put through a fine sieve. Measure the liquid, mix with the honey until finely blended, pour into a bottle, make up to 1pt (600ml) with the whisky, cork tightly.

There is also a version of Athol Brose to be eaten as a sweet course, like Syllabub (p137).

Shrub

1pt (600ml) strained orange juice (or tinned or frozen orange juice) 2lb (900g) crystal sugar
3pt (1.8 litres) rum or brandy

Put the sugar in the orange juice and stand, stirring occasionally, until it is dissolved. Mix with the rum (for Rum Shrub) or the brandy (for Brandy Shrub). Strain through a cloth, bottle and cork tightly.

Sloe Gin

Sloes 1 bottle of gin
Sugar

Pick sloes on a warm sunny day and avoid brushing off the bloom if possible. Pack them into clean warm wine bottles, putting in among them 4oz (110g) sugar to each bottle. The best kind is candy sugar which comes in roughly shaped pieces, but white sugar will do. Fill up with gin. One bottle of gin should do two bottles of sloes. Keep for 6 months or longer.

Blackcurrant Gin

½pt (300ml) measure of good juicy blackcurrants 3oz (90g) sugar
1 bottle of gin

String the blackcurrants and add them with the sugar to the gin. Use a larger bottle for this, eg a cider flagon. Shake it every day until the blackcurrants have broken up and finally become a sediment at the bottom of the bottle. Strain, taste and add more sugar if required, bottle in small bottles and cork securely.

Damson Gin

2lb (900g) damsons   1 quart (1.2 litres) gin
1lb (450g) brown candy sugar or
  barley sugar

Prick the damsons well with a needle, crush the candy, put with the gin into a large screw-topped jar. Shake daily for a month, then strain and bottle. The longer you keep it the better it is.

Curaçao

Rind of 3 Seville oranges   1 bottle (or 1½pt, 900ml)
Rind of 1 lemon   brandy, vodka or aqua vitae
½ tsp coriander seeds   1lb (450g) loaf sugar
¼oz (7g) stick cinnamon   1½pt (900ml) water
A little saffron

Peel the orange and lemon rind very thinly and put it in a large jar. Add the spices and as much saffron as will lie on a five pence piece. Pour the spirit over these, cover closely and keep in a dry warm place for 6 weeks. Then filter through a fine flannel or blotting paper. Boil the sugar and water together, skim and allow to cool. Mix with the filtered spirit. Bottle in small bottles and cork well.

Drambuie

The manufacture of the liqueur Drambuie is a trade secret, but to my palate it appears to be nothing more elaborate than the addition of heather honey to a good malt whisky, probably in the proportion of 1fl oz (30ml) to 1pt (600ml).

Bitters

1oz (30g) Seville orange peel (no   ½oz (15g) crushed gentian root
  white pith)   Brandy to cover
¼oz (7g) shelled and crushed
  cardamoms

Put all ingredients in a jam jar, cover closely and stand for 14 days. Strain through a cloth and put in small bottles—empty liqueur miniatures are suitable. Cork well.

Vermouth

The exact constituents of proprietary vermouths are secrets more closely guarded than the crown jewels, but basically they are fortified wines with added herbs and spices of which wormwood is the principal, and a good appetiser based on wormwood can be made at home. Some of the herbs required can be gathered and dried at any opportunity you may have, and the remainder bought. Always gather herbs on a fine, dry day, when they are just about to flower, and dry them by spreading on sheets of paper on the floor of an airy room. Failing this, hang up in small bunches tied by the stems. The weights given are dried herb weights, and at least twice as much of the fresh herb should be gathered to give this amount. Dry them before use; it takes only a few days in summer weather.

Balm   Bay   Camomile   Fennel

1gal (4.5 litres) ordinary wine (eg a red or white home-made grape wine when ready for use)

1 bottle of the cheapest vodka, or 1pt (600ml) aqua vitae

A saltspoonful each of as many of the following herbs as are obtainable:

gentian	clove
angelica	nutmeg
chamomile	coriander
cinnamon	

2oz (60g) wormwood	½oz (15g) yarrow
½oz (15g) lemon balm	

Sprigs of other herbs may be tried as additions, this is what gives each vermouth its own flavour. Suitable herbs might be:

lavender	ground ivy
rosemary	fennel
sweetbriar	bay leaf
southernwood	pine, fir or spruce
tansy	

Rack off one bottle of the wine for future drinking, and replace it by the bottle of vodka or the aqua vitae. Put the herbs and spices in a cotton bag, put in a jug or deep jar and draw off enough of the wine mixture to cover it well. Cover and leave for 3 days. Then add this essence to the wine mixture, cork and leave a few days before bottling. Costs about one third of a commercial vermouth.

FLAVOURING ESSENCES

The basis of all flavouring essences is to dissolve the essential oils in alcohol, which preserves them and provides a convenient means of handling by using in drops. Many commercial essences are synthetic, and you may like to make some at home so that at least you know you have the real thing. In the case of vanilla, of course, the best cooks keep a special jar of sugar with a vanilla pod in it, and the need for essence is done away with. Almond flavour was obtained by our ancestors by boiling one or two bitter almonds in with the dish, or by using noyau, which is sometimes classed as a liqueur.

Noyau

Keep some stones from good plums (dessert types particularly). Scrub and dry them and put aside until you have enough. Smash them with a hammer and put them in a small screw-top jar which they will fill to one third of its capacity. Fill up with vodka. Screw on the top and leave for 6 months. Strain into small screw-top bottles.

Ratafia

1oz (30g) mixed peach and apricot kernels
4oz (110g) sugar

3 tbsp cold water
¼pt (150ml) brandy

Blanch the kernels by pouring boiling water over them. Put in a screw-top jar. Dissolve the sugar in the water and pour over the kernels, add the brandy which should come to the top of the jar, screw down and store.

Lemon Essence

Peel 3 lemons very thinly, placing the peel in a small screw-top jar. The peel should almost fill the jar. Just cover with vodka, screw down and shake daily for a month. Remove the peel, and bottle the essence in small bottles.

Orange Essence

This is made in exactly the same way as Lemon Essence, using oranges in place of lemons. Oranges and lemons are sometimes dipped in wax preservative by the growers. Spanish, Moroccan or Cypriot fruit is usually untreated. If in any doubt at all, scrub the fruit with hot water to remove the wax.

Garlic Essence

Put 5 or 6 cloves of garlic in a screw-top bottle with a widish neck. The type of small tubby bottle designed to take 25 large tablets or capsules from the chemist's is about right. Fill up the bottle with aqua vitae or vodka and keep for a few weeks. For flavouring soups, stews or salad dressings use 2–3 drops of the essence taken out by means of a steel skewer.

Carlsbad Plums

Save up some screw-top jars (eg honey jars). Pack them three-quarters full, but loosely, with best quality prunes. Cover with any rich red wine of port type (elderberry or beetroot will do). Add one level tablespoon Demerara sugar to each jar, put on cover and keep at least three months—six months is better! These make an instant and most impressive dessert, especially with Cornish cream.

Rum Butter

8oz (230g) unsalted butter
8oz (230g) soft light brown sugar

3fl oz (90ml) rum (marrow rum will do)
A little grated nutmeg

Cream the butter until very light. Gradually work in the sugar alternately with the rum a few drops at a time. Add the nutmeg and beat again. Put into jars or a lidded dish and keep in refrigerator. It keeps for some time. Use as a spread or as a sauce for Christmas pudding, as cake filling or topping.

Brandy Butter

This is made in the same way, using brandy in place of rum. Caster sugar may be used in each case if preferred.

Apple Butter with Cider *(a spread for bread, toast or biscuits)*

1lb (450g) small cooking apples
(well-washed windfalls will do)
½pt (300ml) cider

8oz (230g) soft brown sugar
Pinch each of powdered cinnamon, nutmeg and cloves

Cut up the apples without peeling and simmer in the cider until tender. Put through a sieve. Mix the purée into the sugar, add the spices, put in small pots and leave until cold, cover and tie down the pots and store in a cool dry place.

Pear Honey

Ripe, late pears   Sugar

Peel, core and cut up finely the pears; put in a pan with the same weight of sugar, bring gradually to the boil and simmer about 20 minutes each day for 3 days. Pot, cool and cover.

Country Mincemeat

Make this in an earthenware crock. Begin by chopping finely any sweet dessert apples, such as windfalls or the good parts of faulty apples (discard peels and cores). Put them in layers with demerara sugar sprinkled between. To this add, as they become available, chopped sultanas, raisins, currants or any dried fruit, kernels from stone fruit, and orange and lemon peel finely chopped or minced. Sprinkle in pinches of ground ginger, allspice and cinnamon at intervals. When quinces or japonica fruit are obtainable, grate them in to improve the flavour. Add also bottoms of bottles of home-made wines (exclude the thick lees) until jar is full. Keep well covered throughout. It can be used as required from Christmas till Easter. The last remnants may be too thin for mince pies or tarts, but make excellent Banbury cake filling if thickened with cake crumbs.

Candied Peel

4 oranges
4 lemons
½oz (15g) bicarbonate of soda

1½lb (680g) granulated sugar
¾pt (450ml) water

The best orange peel for candying is from Seville oranges but sweet oranges will do. Save the pulp and juice of the fruit for making Apple and Orange Marmalade (below). Wash the fruit well, cut the lemons lengthwise and oranges crosswise into halves and remove the pulp. Dissolve the bicarbonate of soda in a little hot water, pour it over the peel in the basin. Then add enough water, boiling, to cover the peel entirely and allow to stand for 20 minutes. Pour off, and rinse the peel several times. Put in a saucepan, cover with cold water, bring to the boil and simmer until tender. Strain and replace in basin and cover with fresh cold water. Make a syrup by boiling 1lb (450g) of the sugar with ½pt (300ml) water. Strain peel once more, pour the boiling syrup over it and leave for 2 days. Draw off the syrup and add it to the other ½lb (230g) sugar. Bring to the boil and simmer the peel in it until it looks clear. Take out the peel and dry it on a rack in a very cool oven. Reduce the syrup by boiling it for about half an hour. Dip the peel in it and once more dry in a cool oven. The syrup left over may be beaten up until it is cloudy and thick and then a little may be poured into each cup-shaped piece of candied peel. Store between waxed papers.

Apple and Orange Marmalade

3lb (1.4kg) windfall apples or
  Siberian crabs
Sugar

Orange and/or lemon pulp from
  8 fruits (left over from candied
  peel making)

Wash and cut up the apples. Put in a pan with water barely to cover. Bring to the boil and boil until soft. Strain through a sieve and measure. Add 1lb (450g) of sugar to each 1pt (600ml) of pulp, chop up and add the orange and/or lemon pulp and juice, bring to the boil and simmer for 1½ hours, pot and cover.

5

SYRUPS, SUMMER AND WINTER DRINKS

FRUIT SYRUPS

Syrups, to use diluted with plain or soda water as long summer drinks, or with hot water as a nightcap and cold cure, can be easily made when fruits are obtainable. Though non-alcoholic they keep quite well, but for long keeping (and if an alcohol content is not objectionable) they can be preserved longer by adding ½pt (300ml) of brandy, vodka or whisky to each quart (1.2 litres) of syrup before bottling. The result is strictly called a cordial rather than a syrup. Another good plan is to use fruit bottling jars and sterilise the syrup after boiling. The leftover pulp can be used in Country Wine (p41).

Any of the following fruits are suitable:

blackberries	elderberries
raspberries	bilberries
loganberries	cranberries
mulberries	cherries
currants	plums

Stone the plums or cherries, pick over other fruits. Put the fruit in a jar and stand it in a pan of boiling water until all the juice is given off. Strain and squeeze through a muslin cloth. To each pint (600ml) of juice put 8oz (230g) caster sugar, mix well, bring to the boil and boil for 15 minutes. Skim off any scum as it rises. When cold put in screw-top bottles and make as airtight as possible (eg dip in paraffin wax).

Muscatel Syrup *(very delicious)*

2lb (900g) green gooseberries	½pt (300ml) water
2lb (900g) loaf sugar	2 sprays of elderflowers

Heat the sugar and water, stirring until all is dissolved. Add washed gooseberries. Simmer without breaking the fruit. When gooseberries are soft bring quickly to the boil, plunge in the elderflowers, boil 1 minute only, cool, strain and bottle.

SUMMER DRINKS

The words 'summer drinks' always conjure up for me the thirsty summers of childhood, and so a number of the drinks given here are non-alcoholic. The best of all to me was the wonderful lemonade my mother used to make, given here as Old-fashioned Lemonade. But to an adult palate perhaps fresh lemonade, the *citron pressé* of France, is even more refreshing. Beer and cider both come into the category of summer drinks, though the latter is also an indispensable ingredient of party punches which are good either in summer or winter. There are now good beermaking kits on the market which are quite cheap and convenient, as they save the trouble of shopping for the various ingredients separately. The recipes given are also very good, but you must always remember that home-made beers are approximately twice as strong as commercial beers, so one half pint is like one pint in effect.

Cider can be made at home and I have given recipes for cooking ciders (p69) but it is a dangerous drink for beginners to meddle with; rough cider can have some very bad effects, and some degree of expertise is needed to get a drinkable result. The punch and cup recipes given later are intended to be made with commercial bottled cider.

Beer

This recipe makes a very good pale-coloured beer, rather like lager.

½oz (15g) hops
Water
12oz (350g) crystal malt

8oz (230g) granulated sugar
¾oz (22g) baker's or brewer's yeast

Hops weight very little, and ½oz (15g) is in fact a large handful, so if you are unable to weigh them exactly, one large or two small handfuls is all right. Boil the hops in 1pt (600ml) of water for 10 minutes. Strain off the liquid into a bucket or mash tub and repeat the boiling twice more with the same hops. This extracts the maximum flavour. Stir in the malt and the sugar and make up to 1gal (4.5 litres) with cold water. Add the yeast, cover, and allow to ferment. When the violent fermentation has

died down, after 3–4 days, bottle the beer using small (½pt) beer bottles if possible. The reason for this is that the beer throws a sediment in the bottles, and may be difficult to pour without disturbing this if the bottles are too large. Another way is to bottle in cider flagons and rack off into fresh bottles when the beer has thrown a sediment, putting ½ tsp of sugar in each bottle and keeping another 2–3 weeks in a cool place.

It is ready to drink about a fortnight after bottling but will keep 2–3 months and improve during that time. If a browner beer is preferred, use the same recipe but with 1lb (450g) liquid malt extract instead of 12oz (350g) crystal malt; alternatively use the following recipe for Brown Beer.

Brown Beer

2oz (60g) hops	1½oz (45g) brewer's yeast or
2gal (9 litres) water	equivalent dried yeast
1lb (450g) brown sugar	

Boil the hops in the water for 45 minutes. Add sugar, stir well, and put the liquid through a strainer into a large bucket. When lukewarm add the yeast, cover and ferment for 5 days. Skim carefully and put in a small cask, or bottle straight into beer bottles. Leave for a week before use.

Apple Beer

4lb (1.8kg) apples	2oz (60g) root ginger, bruised
2gal (9 litres) water	1 tsp cloves
3lb (1.4kg) sugar	1 tsp ground cinnamon

Grate the apples and put them in a bucket with the cold water. Cover, and stir every day for a week. Strain on to the sugar and spices. Stir well and leave overnight. Strain again and bottle, corking lightly. Ready for use in a week.

Ginger Beer

2lb (900g) sugar	½oz (15g) essence of ginger
½oz (15g) tartaric acid	2gal (9 litres) water
½oz (15g) cream of tartar	1oz (30g) yeast

Put the sugar in a bucket with the tartaric acid, cream of tartar and ginger essence. Pour on 1gal (4.5 litres) boiling water and stir until dissolved. Add another gallon (4.5 litres) of cold water. When lukewarm add the yeast. Let it stand, covered, until quite cold. Bottle in strong bottles and tie down the corks, or use screw-top cider bottles, or ginger beer bottles with patent tops. Keep about a week.

Ginger Pop

1oz (30g) whole ginger	2 tsp fresh yeast or equivalent
½oz (15g) cream of tartar	dried yeast
12oz (350g) loaf sugar	Slice of toast
1gal (4.5 litres) water	

Bruise the ginger and put in a bucket with cream of tartar and sugar. Pour on the water, boiling. Cover and leave until lukewarm. Add the yeast spread on toast, cover and leave 24 hours. Strain through muslin and put in strong screw-top bottles. Use after 3 days.

Lemon Ginger Beer

This was a famous haymaking drink in the countryside. The use of ginger in cold drinks for thirsty workers in hot weather was supposed to prevent a chill to the stomach and enable them to quench their thirst more amply.

3 lemons	2oz (60g) cream of tartar
3lb (1.4kg) sugar	2gal (9 litres) boiling water
2oz (60g) whole ginger, bruised	1oz (30g) yeast on toast

Peel the lemon rinds thinly. Squeeze the juice. Put the rinds and juice in a bucket with the sugar, ginger and cream of tartar. Pour over 2gal (9 litres) boiling water. When lukewarm add yeast spread on toast. Let it ferment 24 hours, then strain and bottle as for ginger beer.

Nettle Beer

Pick the nettles when young, well before they flower, and measure slightly pressed down.

1gal (4.5 litres) nettles	1½oz (45g) bruised whole ginger
1gal (4.5 litres) water	1 tsp cream of tartar
2 lemons	1oz (30g) yeast
1lb (450g) sugar	

Boil the nettles in the water for 15 minutes. Put the sugar, thinly peeled lemon rinds, lemon juice, ginger, and cream of tartar in a bucket. If liked, add a bunch of pineapple mint or a bunch of lemon balm, well bruised. Pour on the boiling nettle liquor, strained, making up to 1gal (4.5 litres) with water if necessary. When lukewarm add the yeast. Cover and leave for 24 hours. Skim, strain and bottle as for Ginger Beer. Ready in 2–3 days.

Elderflower Lemonade
Sometimes called 'Elderflower Champagne', but lemonade is the more accurate description.

1pt (600ml) elderflower heads	1½lb (680g) loaf sugar
(loosely packed)	2 lemons
1gal (4.5 litres) water	2 tbsp white wine vinegar

Boil the water and pour over the sugar, mix well. When cool add flower heads, vinegar and lemon, sliced. Cover and stand for 24 hours. Strain and bottle at once in cider or champagne bottles, and lay the bottles on their sides in a cold place. Drink after 3 weeks.

Old-Fashioned Lemonade

2 lemons	1 quart (1.2 litres) boiling water
2oz (60g) sugar	

Scrub the lemons and slice thinly with a stainless knife, on a plate so as not to waste any juice. Put the slices and juice into an earthenware jug. Add sugar and boiling water and cool. When cold, place in a fridge or cool place overnight. Strain and serve.

Fresh Lemonade
Allow 1 large lemon and 1oz (30g) sugar to 1pt (600ml) of cold water and chill in a refrigerator, or use less water and add some ice cubes. Squeeze or liquidise the lemon.

Lemon Cooler

Juice of 1 lemon
1 egg
½ teacup water

2 tbsp shaved or well-crushed ice
Soda water
Slice of lemon

Put all the ingredients except soda water and slice of lemon into a cocktail shaker and shake well for a few minutes until the ice is melted (or put in a food mixer, or beat with a rotary whisk). Strain into a tumbler, fill up with soda water, put a slice of lemon on top and serve with straws. Can also be made with orange or grapefruit. This is a good disguise for a nourishing drink for invalids and convalescents.

Cider Punch

2 large oranges
1 tbsp Demerara sugar
1 wineglass orange curaçao
2 1pt (600ml) tins pineapple juice

2 flagons medium sweet cider
2 rosy apples
About 1pt (600ml) sparkling bitter lemon

Wash the oranges and slice them thinly into a large china punch bowl. Sprinkle them with the sugar and pour on the orange curaçao. Leave, covered with a plate, for about 8 hours. Then pour on the pineapple juice and the cider. Wash the apples, do not peel them but quarter, core and slice thinly. Float them in the punch. Just before serving pour in the bitter lemon. If none is available use the juice of a lemon or 1 tbsp bottled lemon juice and add a syphonful of soda water.

This is a particularly delicious and refreshing drink for parties, either summer or winter. Serve in small glasses (3fl oz [90ml] size).

Fruit Punch *(non-alcoholic)*

A delicious adaptation of the recipe above to suit occasions when alcohol would be inappropriate.

1 orange
A sprinkling of caster sugar
1–2 tsp sherry, madeira or home-made currant wine
1pt (600ml) tinned orange juice

1pt (600ml) tinned pineapple juice
1 rosy apple
2 11oz (330ml) tins aerated bitter lemon

Scrub the orange and slice thinly. Sprinkle with sugar and wine, cover and marinate for some hours in a fridge or cool place. Put the tins of fruit juice and bitter lemon in the fridge. When required, put the orange and its juices into punch bowl, add the orange and pineapple juice, quarter, core and thinly slice the apple in; finally add the bitter lemon and serve.

Pudge

4 oranges	2 bottles white wine (elderflower
2 lemons	will do)
4 apples	2 flagons medium sweet cider
4oz (110g) brown sugar	1 banana (optional)
¼ bottle brandy	Soda water

Wash the fruit carefully and cut the oranges and lemons into thin slices and each slice into four sections. Put in china punch bowl. Core the apples but do not peel, and cut into thin segments. Add to the oranges and lemons, sprinkling brown sugar over them. Cover and leave for several hours or overnight. Then add the brandy, wine and cider. Just before serving slice in the banana if liked, and add a syphon of soda water.

Claret Cooler *(a claret cup)*

A bottle of claret	Ice cubes
4fl oz (120ml) orange juice	1 quart (1.2 litres) soda water (2
4fl oz (120ml) lemon juice	syphonfuls)
4fl oz (120ml) sugar syrup	Orange, lemon and peach slices

Make the syrup in advance by boiling 1lb (450g) sugar in 1pt (600ml) water for 10 minutes, and bottling for use.

Mix the claret, fruit juices and syrup in punch bowl or large pitcher. Add ice cubes and soda water, garnish with the fruit.

Hock Sparkler *(a hock cup)*

3 bottles hock	1 liqueur glass brandy
1lb (450g) sliced pineapple or	3 liqueur glasses orange curaçao
peaches (fresh or tinned)	Soda water
Caster sugar	

Slice the fruit thinly and sprinkle with sugar to taste (or put tinned fruit and juice in bowl without sugar). Add the hock and chill for 1 hour. Chill the brandy and curaçao separately. Just before serving stir them into the rest, add a syphon of soda water and put an ice cube in each glass.

Cider Cup

4pt (2.25 litres) cider	Strained juice of 4 oranges
2pt (1.2 litres) fizzy lemonade	Strained juice of 4 lemons
½pt (300ml) cold water	8oz (230g) caster sugar

Mix all the ingredients in a large jug or punch bowl. Leave in a cold place for 2 hours. Decorate with borage leaves and flowers, or with thinly sliced cucumber and whole mint leaves. Serve with ice cubes.

Mint Julep

One of the world's famous drinks that originated in the United States, and the presentation, in plain glass tumblers, is part and parcel of the drink. First of all, the edges of the glasses must be frosted. The glasses must be perfectly clean and dry; have in front of you two saucers, one with a little cold water and the other

containing caster sugar. Dip the rim of each glass in the water and then into the sugar and twist it around a few times until nicely frosted with the sugar. Set aside in a cool place.

Now assemble the following ingredients:

fresh garden mint	Bourbon whisky
caster sugar	orange and lemon slices
soda water	Maraschino cherries
crushed ice	

Work neatly so as not to disturb the frosting. Into each glass put a few mint leaves and 1 tsp sugar, and prod with a swizzle stick or long spoon to bruise the leaves. Add a splash of soda and then almost fill the glass with crushed ice. Add 1½fl oz (45ml) whisky. If possible, frost the outside of the glass by setting it in a container of crushed ice and stirring the contents briskly to freeze the outside. Set an orange slice and a lemon slice on the edge of the glass, put one or two sprigs of mint and a cherry in the top, and serve. If no Bourbon is obtainable use any whisky, or try your carrot whisky if you like!

Tom Collins

2 tsp caster sugar	1½fl oz (45ml) gin
Juice of 1 lemon	Soda water
Crushed ice	Maraschino cherry

Put the lemon juice and sugar in a glass, add one third of a glass crushed ice and pour the gin over it. Top up the glass with soda water and serve with cherry.

Planter's Punch

1fl oz (30ml) lemon juice or lime juice	Tumblerful of crushed ice
	Slice of orange, slice of lemon,
1 tsp sugar	cherry, sprig of mint or borage
1fl oz (30ml) Jamaica rum	

Combine all the ingredients except garnishes in a shaker or a jug and shake or stir well, pour into 10fl oz (300ml) glass, garnish with the orange, lemon, cherry and mint or borage, and serve.

Cuba Libre

Ice

1½fl oz (45ml) rum

1 tsp lime juice

Coca-cola

Put ice in a tall glass, add rum and lime juice, and top up with Coca-cola.

TEETOTAL PUNCHES

The Americans are particularly good at non-alcoholic drinks, and the following fruit punches are delicious and health-giving.

Punch Base

This mixture is basic to all the punches, giving them the necessary tang. American cup measure is 8fl oz (240ml).

1 cup orange juice

½ cup lemon juice

1 cup sugar

2 cups water

Grated rinds of ½ orange and 1 lemon

Pineapple Punch

1 cup grated pineapple or an 8oz (230g) tin crushed pineapple

A 1pt (600ml) syphon of soda water

Add the pineapple to the punch base and add soda water just before serving. Serves 8–10 large glasses.

Grape-Ginger Punch

4 cups (about 1½pt or about 900ml) grape juice

4 cups (4 small bottles) ginger ale

2 syphons soda water

Add all to punch base and serve at once.

Orange Ice Punch

1pt (600ml) orange juice

4pt (2.25 litres or 3 large bottles) aerated orange drink

1 cup crushed pineapple

4oz (110g) stoned fresh cherries

Add to punch base and chill before serving.

Apple Juice and Soda

1pt (600ml) tinned apple juice   Soda water
Ice cubes

Put 2–3 ice cubes in each glass, add apple juice to two-thirds full and top up with soda water.

Apple Lemonade

1 quart (1.2 litres) apple juice   Sugar to taste
1 cup lemon juice

Mix all together and serve with ice and sprigs of mint in the glasses.

Apple Drink

Windfalls, or even cores and peelings, can be used to make a refreshing summer drink which is especially appreciated by children and invalids.

Wash and slice 3 medium-sized apples, windfalls, or the equivalent amount of waste. Put in a jug and pour on a quart (1.2 litres) of boiling water. Cover and stand until cold. Sweeten to taste and chill before serving.

Almost any other fruit can be used in a similar way.

WINTER DRINKS

Hot Rumour

1 orange   3 tbsp Demerara rum
12 cloves   4 level tbsp Demerara sugar
1 bottle claret or home-made red
  wine

Stick the orange with the cloves, wrap in cooking foil and bake for 30 minutes in a moderate oven, 350°F (180°C), Gas 4. Heat the wine in a saucepan almost to boiling point, then add rum and sugar. Float the orange on top and poach gently for 10 minutes. Serve the drink hot with the orange still floating in the bowl.

Madison Mull

1 apple	1 bottle red wine
6 cloves	2 level tbsp sugar
1pt (600ml) dry vintage cider	

Stud the apple with cloves and bake in a moderate oven, 350°F (180°C), Gas 4 for 30 minutes. Heat the cider to near boiling point, put in apple, add red wine and sugar, reheat but do not allow to boil, and simmer for a few minutes. Strain into bowl and serve hot.

Dutch Rum Punch
Easy to memorise as each quantity doubles the previous one.

One sour (lemon, thin peel and juice)	**Four** strong (4 tbsp rum)
Two sweet (2 tbsp sugar)	**Eight** weak (boiling water, 8 tbsp or 4fl oz 120ml)

Add sweet to sour, add strong to both, pour weak over all.

Marrow Rum Punch

Thinly peeled rind and juice of 1 lemon	2fl oz (60ml) marrow rum
	Hot water

Put the peel, juice and rum in a heatproof 8fl oz (240ml) tumbler and pour on hot water to fill.

Mulled Cider *(serves 12)*

3 quarts (3.5 litres) cider	1 tsp allspice
½ cup brown sugar (4oz, 110g)	2in (5cm) stick cinnamon
1 tsp cloves	1 tsp nutmeg

Put everything except the nutmeg in a large pan and simmer for 15 minutes. Add nutmeg and serve hot.

Mulled Wine

½pt (300ml) elderberry wine (or damson or other rich red wine)	A piece of ginger
½pt (300ml) boiling water	2 tsp sugar
6 cloves	Thinly peeled rind of a lemon
	Dash of ground nutmeg

Boil the cloves, ginger and sugar in the water for 1 minute. Add the lemon peel, nutmeg and wine and reheat gently but do not boil.

Captain's Cup

1 bottle red wine	2 tbsp sugar
1 tsp ground cinnamon	2–3 tbsp brandy
3 cloves	½pt (300ml) boiling water

Put wine and spices in a pan and bring just to the boil. Add sugar, boiling water and brandy, and serve hot.

Claret cup

1 quart (1.2 litres) claret (or home-made red wine)	1pt (600ml) water
	1 liqueur glass orange curaçao
2 sliced oranges	1 wineglass brandy
Sugar	Nutmeg
6 cloves	

Place wine, oranges, sugar to taste and cloves in a saucepan. Bring almost to boil. Boil 1pt (600ml) water in a kettle and add gradually to mixture. Add curaçao and brandy. Pour into mugs or glasses and grate a little nutmeg on top. Makes 24 punch glasses (or coffee cups 'demi-tasse' size).

Apple Toddy

Mix equal quantities of boiling water and tinned apple juice or pineapple juice and take at bedtime for a cold. Alternatively heat up home-made Apple Drink (p 95).

The Flaming Punch Bowl

1 bottle red wine	Juice of 1 orange
1 bay leaf (torn in pieces)	Juice of ½ lemon
½ tsp mixed spice	A miniature of brandy (or a small
1 sliced whole orange	wineglassful)

Put the wine and all the other ingredients except the brandy into a pan and heat until very hot but not quite boiling. Pour into punch bowl. Warm the brandy separately until fairly hot, pour it carefully over the surface of the punch, set alight immediately and ladle the punch into serving glasses.

Tom and Jerry
A famous American drink for parties. Assemble ingredients before starting.

1 egg to each 2 people
Sugar
Bicarbonate of soda
1 tbsp each rum and brandy per
 person

1 cup milk per person (heating in
 readiness)
Nutmeg

Separate the eggs, beat the whites until stiff, fold in 1½ tsp caster sugar for each egg. Beat the yolks and then add to the whites, beating to a smooth batter. Add a pinch of bicarbonate of soda and keep well stirred during serving. Put 1 tbsp of batter in each mug, and 1 tbsp rum and 1 tbsp brandy (mixed ready). Fill up with hot milk, stir, and sprinkle grated nutmeg on top.

Milk Punch

1 bottle rum
4 lemons
2 or 3 bitter almonds if available, or plum kernels or Ratafia (p80)

½ bottle sherry or sherry-type wine, not too sweet
2lb (900g) loaf sugar
¾pt (450ml) milk

Peel the lemons thinly, put the peel and the bitter almonds or equivalent in a small jar and cover with rum, put on cover or top and leave for 3 days, stirring daily. Mix together the rest of the rum, the wine and the sugar, and strain in the lemon flavoured rum. Boil the milk and pour into the mixture through a strainer. Cover and let it stand for 2 hours. Then strain into small bottles using a straining cloth inside a funnel. Cork well and leave for 6 months before use.

As this can be made in summertime the surplus lemon juice can be used at once for fresh lemonade or made into a syrup with 8oz (230g) sugar (for method see Fruit Syrups, p84) and kept for winter use as hot lemon, etc.

6

COUNTRY REMEDIES
AND HERB TEAS

There are many traditional country remedies for minor ailments such as colds which are at best as effective as 'something from the chemist's' and at the very least pleasant and harmless. At the time of writing more serious conditions are in the hands of specialist medicine, at least in Western Europe; but we cannot know if there may be a time when some breakdown of civilisation might make it necessary to revive the ancient lore of herbs and simple remedies, for use in emergency in even the worst diseases.

Blackberry Cordial *(colds, sore throats)*

1 quart (1.2 litres) ripe blackberries
1pt (600ml) white wine vinegar

1lb (450g) loaf sugar
8 oz (230g) honey

Put the blackberries in an earthenware jar, pour over the vinegar, cover and let it stand for 7–8 days to extract the juice, stirring daily. When ready, strain it on to the sugar and honey in a saucepan. Bring to the boil, allow to get cold, bottle and cork well. Keep it in a dark place or cover bottles with brown paper wrappers. Dose: 1 tbsp in a glass of hot water.

Raspberry Vinegar *(sore throats)*

2 quarts (2.25 litres) raspberries   Loaf sugar
1pt (600ml) white wine vinegar

Put the raspberries and vinegar in an earthenware jar and extract juice for 7–8 days as in the last recipe. Strain and measure the liquid and allow 1lb (450g) loaf sugar for every pint (600ml). Boil up, cool and bottle. Dose: 1 tbsp in a glass of hot water.

Strawberry Vinegar

1 quart (1.2 litres) strawberries   1lb (450g) white sugar to each
1 quart (1.2 litres) white wine   1pt (600ml) of juice
vinegar

Cover the strawberries with the vinegar, cover and stand 6 days, pressing and squeezing daily. Strain and measure the juice. Add required sugar, bring to the boil and boil for 5 minutes only, longer boiling may cause the vinegar to jelly. Cool and bottle. Good for sore throats, or as an emergency sweet sauce for puddings or ice cream.

Nettle Syrup

This old recipe is a fine blood tonic. Gather the tips of young nettles, wash well. To every 1lb (450g) nettles put 1 quart (1.2 litres) water, and boil for 1 hour. Strain and measure, add 1lb (450g) sugar to each pint (600ml) of juice, boil for 30 minutes, cool and bottle. Dilute to taste with water or soda water. Dose: 1 tbsp.

Rose Syrup *(sore throats, pick-me-up)*

1lb (450g) rhubarb   12oz (350g) white sugar
1pt (600ml) cold water   Petals of 7 red roses (large double)

Cut up and simmer the rhubarb in the water until very soft. Strain and add the sugar and rose petals, simmer 15 minutes, strain again and simmer until syrup thickens and is a rich red colour. Pour into dry, clean, warmed jars and seal securely. Dose: 1 tsp diluted with 1 tbsp boiling water in a mug; let it cool and then fill up with cold milk.

Treacle Posset

A sure cold cure if taken early enough at onset; half these quantities may do.

1pt milk

2 tbsp treacle

Juice of 1 lemon

The treacle in this recipe may be black cooking treacle or golden syrup; black molasses as sold in health food shops is too strong. Put milk in a saucepan and bring almost to boiling point. Add treacle and lemon juice and simmer until the curd separates. Strain through a muslin in a funnel, and serve hot.

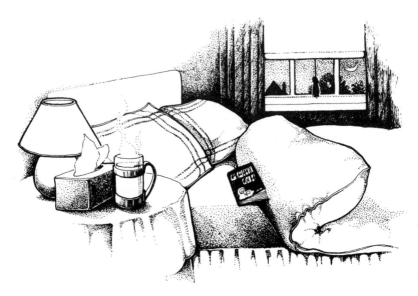

Treacle Hot Milk

A good comforter for a cold, a variant on the above, is to take a glass of hot milk well sweetened with golden syrup at bedtime.

Sunflower Seed Cordial *(for bronchitis)*

1oz (30g) sunflower seeds

1 quart (1.2 litres) cold water

2 tbsp sugar or honey

Put the sunflower seeds and water in a saucepan, bring to the boil, simmer slowly until liquid is reduced to 1pt. Strain and sweeten with sugar or honey. Bottle and cork well. Dose: 1 tbsp when cough becomes troublesome.

Black Rob *(for breaking up a cold)*

Blackcurrants	Root ginger
Cloves	Sugar
Cassia buds	A little brandy

Extract the juice from the blackcurrants by putting them in a jar or basin in a pan of boiling water. Crush with a wooden spoon. When juice is all drawn off, strain and measure. To each pint (600ml) add 1lb (450g) sugar and $1/6$oz (5g) each of cloves, cassia buds and bruised ginger. Bring gradually to the boil. Boil for 5 minutes, cool, add 1 tbsp brandy and bottle. Dose: 1fl oz (2 tbsp or 30ml) in a glass of hot water.

Red Rob *(colds)*

Ripe elderberries   Water

To every 1 pt (600ml) juice allow:

$1/6$oz (5g) each of cloves, cassia   1lb (450g) sugar
 buds and root ginger

Strip the elderberries from their stalks, just cover with water, simmer for 20 minutes. Strain and measure, add rest of ingredients, boil for 10 minutes. Don't overboil or it will jelly. Cool, strain and bottle. Dose: 1fl oz (30ml) in hot water at bedtime.

Grapefruit and Orange Compound *(for rheumatism sufferers)*

3 grapefruit	2oz (60g) Epsom Salts
3 oranges	2oz (60g) cream of tartar
3 lemons	1pt (600ml) boiling water

Squeeze the juice from all the fruit. Put the skins and pulp through a mincer (or put whole fruit through liquidiser). Stand overnight. On the second day, strain and squeeze juice through muslin. Dissolve Epsom Salts and cream of tartar in the boiling water and add the juice. Put in bottles, stirring to keep the cream

of tartar in suspension. Cool well, store in cool place. Dose: ½ wineglass (2fl oz or 60ml) before breakfast daily for 6 months.

Face Lotion or After-Shave

6 ripe ridge cucumbers ½pt (300ml) distilled rose water
½ drachm (1.5ml) powdered 25 drops tincture of benzoin
  borax (¼ tsp)

Cut up the cucumbers into ½in (12mm) slices, put into a steamer and steam until soft. Squeeze the pulp through fairly coarse muslin. Measure, and for every 3fl oz (90ml) allow the above rose water and other ingredients. Dissolve the borax in the rose water, and add the benzoin drop by drop, shaking the bottle at intervals. Pour this mixture over the cucumber pulp, stir thoroughly and bottle securely. Keeps well.

HERB TEAS

For some reason, many people quail at the mention of herb tea whereas they will lap it up quite happily if you call it a tisane. In either case, it is an infusion of some leaf, flower or seed, and anyway the tea we all drink daily is itself a herbal infusion made from the dried leaves of *Camellia sinensis*. Our ancestors used herb teas extensively for thirst-quenching as well as for their medicinal or dietetic value, and we miss a great deal by not doing likewise.

The essential thing is that herbs for tea should be gathered at the right time (a dry sunny morning just before they flower is usual) and dried before use. Hill's *Herbal*, a family standby of the early 1800s, says they should be spread on the floor of a dry airy room (on sheets of brown paper, one must add). A better method is to spread them on muslin-covered cake racks and put them in a current of warm air such as over a hot-water tank or in an airing cupboard. The quicker they dry the better they are, and they should dry green.

When the herbs are dry they are mostly powdered or at least broken up by rolling between the palms of the hands (exceptions are noted in the recipes), put in a paper bag and then into an airtight container. It's a good idea to save screw-top jars for this, or tins with well-fitting lids. Label clearly.

Unless otherwise stated most herb teas require about ½oz (15g) of dried herb to 1pt (600ml) boiling water. Make them in a small teapot or covered jug. Heat the pot, make sure the water is really boiling, and let the herb infuse for about 10 minutes before straining into cups. Sugar, honey or saccharin may be added if you enjoy the tea better sweetened; and many herb teas, as well as being drunk hot, can be cooled and finally chilled before drinking, and are very refreshing in hot weather.

The great advantage of herb teas is that in most cases they need cost nothing except the trouble of gathering and drying! You may not have access to brooklime or centaury, but many gardens contain sage, mint, balm and thyme, four of the most valuable herbs for teas. Bramble leaf tea is an excellent daily drink.

Agrimony Tea
Excellent for the liver, good for coughs and a good blood tonic.

Balm Tea
Good for fevers, colds, headache and nervousness. Aids digestion. Make it from dried leaves, although it can also be made from fresh leaves especially in the month of May. An old gardener once recited to me:

> *He who drinks the balm in May*
> *Will live for ever and a day.*

I was impressed, as he was 83 years of age, but an element of doubt crept in when another old gardener repeated exactly the same rhyme except that 'sage' replaced 'balm'. Perhaps one should drink both balm tea and sage tea in May to be on the safe side. Drying time is July.

Betony Tea
A tonic herb, sometimes drunk by country people as a tea substitute.

Blackberry (Bramble Leaf) Tea
Mildly astringent and tonic (therein resembling Indian tea); the young leaves dried as described make a very good substitute for Indian tea. The medicinal action of blackberry tea is so mild it can be drunk day in and day out with only beneficial effects. An English mixed herb tea can be made with bramble leaf, betony and couch grass, but the latter gives it a milky flavour not to everyone's taste. Bramble leaf alone is a pleasantly palatable drink.

Brooklime Tea
For kidneys, bladder and blood. Brooklime *(Veronica beccabunga)* is a little blue flower of the speedwell family, which can also be eaten fresh in salads as it is rich in Vitamin C and somewhat resembles watercress.

Camomile Tea
The dried flowers are used, 20 flowers to 1pt (600ml) of water. Supposed to be good for indigestion if taken first thing in the morning.

Centaury Tea
Bitter, but an excellent general tonic and very good for attacks of biliousness.

Coltsfoot Tea
Young leaves and flowers (dried) for coughs. Flowers alone, tonic.

106

Camomile   *Lime flower*   *Peppermint*

Elderflower Tea
For fevers, colds and insomnia. Pick the flowers when just out, cutting immediately below the flower head, dry and store. Taken hot at night it induces sweating, and is a very good cure for colds and flu in place of aspirin.

Germander Tea
From woodsage or wood germander *(Teucrium scorodonia)* or wall germander *(T. chamaedrys)*, for gout and rheumatism.

From water germander *(T. scordium)*, said to be good in fevers as a sudorific.

107

Ground Ivy Tea

Use 1oz (30g) of dried ground ivy to 1pt (600ml) of boiling water, sweeten it with honey, and take for coughs and as a general blood purifier and tonic. May be drunk daily if you like for general health.

Groundsel Tea

Boil a handful of groundsel in a quart (1.2 litres) of water for 20 minutes. Drink a wineglassful each morning to help ease backache.

Hop Tea

Half an ounce (15g) to 1pt (600ml), a famous remedy for insomnia.

Lime Flower Tea

For headaches and insomnia.

Marigold Tea

Dry the petals only. General tonic. Can be drunk as often as you like.

Marjoram Tea

Good for indigestion. A sprig of marjoram placed beside a jug of milk was said to keep it fresh.

Mint Tea

Use fresh or dried. A pleasant drink and excellent digestive, good for biliousness.

Periwinkle Tea

Leaves only, preferably use fresh. A quick pick-me-up and nerve tonic.

Peppermint Tea

Has similar properties to spearmint (Mint Tea, above). To get the best flavour from peppermint, the leaves should be left whole after drying.

Raspberry Leaf Tea
Tea made from dried raspberry leaves is very good for the kidneys as well as possessing its well-known prenatal value. Very good iced. As a prenatal drink take 1pt (600ml) daily from four months of pregnancy onward.

Rosemary Tea
Good for colds, headaches and stomach aches.

Sage Tea
Tonic. Sage contains a natural antiseptic and is also a good gargle for sore throats.

Thyme Tea
For colds and indigestion.

Yarrow Tea
For colds, fevers, diarrhoea, bladder infections.

7

USING HOME-MADE WINES IN COOKERY

The use of wine in cooking is now so widespread that it really needs no introduction; it is only necessary to point out that home-made wines turn commonplace dishes into something special exactly as grape wines do. In the same way, ends of bottles or odd amounts left over at bottling time can be used up in cooking, as can any of your less successful wines.

Almost all soups and stews are improved by the addition of a dash of wine, and it can replace stock or water in savoury recipes and water or fruit juice in sweet ones. The recipes in the following pages are intended to start you off experimenting; obviously the list could be much extended, but I have included a few each of meat, fish, savoury and sweet dishes, and some miscellaneous oddments. Once the habit of cooking with wine is acquired you will wonder how you managed without it, and if you use your own wines the cost is trifling.

To avoid lengthy lists of possible wines to use in each dish I have simply described them as red or white, dry or sweet, and left it to the cook to decide among elderberry, beetroot, plum, bramble, elderflower, gorse, potato or whatever might be available. Where a red grape wine is really unobtainable for some classic dish like Coq au Vin the best substitute is Romany Claret (p60).

In all recipes containing flour, plain flour is intended.

SOUPS

The wines mentioned in most cookery books as suitable for use in soups are Burgundy, Bordeaux (red and white), sherry and Marsala, and home-made wines should be chosen to approximate to these types. Celery wine is particularly good in both soups and stews as it retains and imparts the celery flavour.

Cream of Mushroom Soup *(serves 2–3)*
Mushrooms and wine seem to have an affinity, and as mushrooms appear fairly frequently in these recipes it may be worth mentioning that they need not always be expensive. Button mushrooms are only required where stated, otherwise field mushrooms are as good or better. Again, you may be able to grow your own, or if you have access to countryside and are confident that you know your fungi, the edible brown boletus or 'penny bun' makes an excellent substitute in all mushroom dishes. It is said that this fungus, once plentiful in woods round London, had disappeared completely through being over-picked by enthusiastic members of the French and Italian communities of Soho. The 'penny bun' is particularly good in soups such as the following:

For the base

1oz (30g) butter	¾pt (450ml) milk
1 tbsp flour	Salt and pepper

For the rest

4oz (110g) mushrooms, chopped finely	1 tbsp sherry-type wine
	1 tsp chopped parsley
1oz (30g) butter	A little grated nutmeg
Dash of garlic (1 clove or 2–3 drops essence)	Salt and pepper
	¼pt (150ml) chicken stock

111

First make the base by putting all the ingredients into a small pan and at once stirring rapidly and continuously over moderate heat until it thickens. Cook for 2–3 minutes, stirring. Keep hot over a pan of hot water. In another saucepan heat the butter, add garlic (if a clove is used remove after 1 minute). Add the chopped mushrooms and cook gently until tender. Add the wine, bring to the boil, reduce heat, add parsley and seasonings, simmer for 5 minutes and then add the chicken stock. Bring to boil again, stir in the base, when thoroughly blended serve at once.

Minestrone Soup *(serves 4–6)*

This soup is made without wine and is delicious in itself, and if enough is made for two days it can be turned into Portuguese soup on the second day with the aid of any rosé type of wine, such as Tutti-frutti (p63) or Bramble (p37).

A handful each of chopped carrot, chopped swede, chopped turnip, chopped potato, chopped onion and chopped celery

1 or 2 tomatoes, chopped, if available

¼ small white cabbage, savoy or cauliflower, finely shredded (outside leaves will do if coarsest parts are discarded)

3oz (90g) margarine

Salt and pepper

4pt (2.4 litres) water heated to boiling point

5oz (140g) tomato purée, or tinned tomatoes well chopped or put through a food-mixer (1lb tin or nearest size available)

2oz (60g) long grain rice or 2oz (60g) spaghetti broken small

A pinch basil or oregano

A bayleaf

The ingredients may be varied according to season but must always include tomatoes or tomato purée, some member of the cabbage family, and rice or spaghetti. To obtain the characteristic appearance and texture of this soup the vegetables must be chopped neatly into ¼in (6mm) cubes. Large or rough pieces spoil its appetising appearance.

Melt the margarine in a large saucepan and throw in the chopped onion, followed by the other chopped vegetables with the exception of the cabbage. Shake over heat for a few minutes to bring out the flavour but do not allow to brown. Season with salt and pepper and pour on the water, boiling. Return to the boil and cook rapidly for 15–20 minutes. Add the shredded

cabbage, the tomato purée, and the rice or spaghetti in small handfuls. When boiling again add the basil or oregano and the bayleaf. Reduce heat and cook gently until rice or pasta is tender. Taste and adjust seasoning. Served with bread and cheese, it makes a complete meal.

Any leftover minestrone can be used as follows:

Portuguese Soup *(serves 2–3)*

A small onion	A beef stock cube
Leftover minestrone (about 1pt or 600ml)	½ tsp curry powder
	Gravy browning
A little green pepper	Rosé wine

Chop the onion finely and brown it well in a little fat or cooking oil. With a fork, or pastry blender, mash the vegetables in the cold minestrone. Pour on to the onion, bring to the boil, add some chopped green pepper or 1 tsp dehydrated mixed pepper, 1 beef stock cube, the curry powder, and enough gravy browning to make a good rich brown colour. Simmer for 15 minutes. Just before serving add a wineglassful of rosé (or white) wine.

Brown Lentil Soup *(serves 6)*

This delicious and nourishing Italian soup must be made with whole lentils, which have dingy brownish skins, not the more common orange-coloured dried lentils.

8oz (230g) brown lentils
1 onion, finely chopped
1 clove garlic, crushed
1 heaped tbsp finely chopped parsley
4 tbsp olive oil

1 12oz tin tomatoes (or nearest size obtainable)
Salt and pepper
1 wineglass red (or celery) wine wine

Cook the lentils in 2 quarts (2.25 litres) of boiling, lightly salted water for 1 hour. Strain the liquid into a jug and set aside the lentils. Put the onion, garlic and parsley into the saucepan, pour the lentil liquor over them, bring to the boil and when boiling fast add the olive oil and continue to boil briskly for 10 minutes. Mash or purée the tomatoes, add to the pan, replace the lentils, add pepper and salt to taste, and cook gently for 20 minutes. Add the wine, stir and serve.

Oxtail Soup *(serves 4–6)*

1 oxtail
A few sticks of celery
1 large carrot
1 large onion
2oz (60g) dripping or other fat
2 quarts (2.5 litres) stock (beef or bone stock, or made with cubes)
4oz (125g) lean ham or a ham or bacon bone

¼ tsp mixed herbs, 1 bay leaf, 2 cloves and 6 peppercorns, all tied in muslin
1½oz (45g) flour
Salt and pepper
½ lemon or 2 tsp lemon juice
1 tbsp strong red or sherry-type wine

Get your butcher to chop the oxtail, wash it thoroughly and divide it into joints. Clean and slice the vegetables. Put the meat into cold water, bring to the boil, then strain it and dry it. Melt the dripping in a large, thick pan, fry the meat until brown all over, add the vegetables and fry lightly, then add the stock, ham and bag of herbs. Simmer for 5 hours. Strain off the liquor, leaving a little with the meat and vegetables and set them aside for later use (see Oxtail Casserole, p115). Skim the fat off the liquor and put the latter into another saucepan. Blend the flour with the cold water and stir into the soup while bringing it to the boil. Taste for seasoning and add salt and pepper if required, then the lemon juice. Cook for 5 minutes and add the wine just before serving.

MEAT DISHES

Oxtail Casserole *(serves 4)*
The chef of a famous hotel divulged that the secret of his superb oxtail was that he cooked it all day, every day for three days!

A medium-sized onion	Meat and vegetables left over
1oz (30g) butter or dripping	from Oxtail Soup (kept over-
2 tsp flour	night)
10fl oz (400ml) beef stock	A wineglass of red or sherry-type
	wine

Chop the onion finely and fry it in the fat until brown but not burnt. Stir in the flour and add the stock, bring to the boil while stirring. If the stock is not made with beef cubes, adjust the seasoning with salt and pepper and add a few drops of gravy browning. Put this sauce into the pan with the oxtail and simmer the whole very gently for 5–6 hours with the lid on. Cool and set aside overnight. Next day simmer gently for another 5–6 hours, or put it in a casserole in a very slow oven—225°F (110°C), Gas ¼—for the same length of time. Stir in the wine an hour before serving.

Beef Casserole with Mushrooms *(serves 5–6)*

2lb (900g) beef (topside or chuck steak)	¼pt (150ml) dry red wine
	Pinch of thyme
1½oz (45g) cooking fat	Bayleaf
6–12 shallots or small onions	1 clove garlic
4oz (110g) thick rashers streaky bacon	Salt and pepper
	4oz (110g) small mushrooms
1 level tbsp flour	A little butter
¼pt (150ml) stock (stock cube)	

Trim the meat and cut into cubes (not too small). Melt the cooking fat in a frying pan and quickly brown the meat all over. Lift out with a perforated spoon and place in a casserole. Peel the shallots and brown in the fat. Add to the meat. Dice the bacon and fry in the same fat. Sprinkle in the flour, stirring. When it browns stir in the stock and the wine. Bring to the boil. Add thyme, bayleaf, crushed garlic and seasoning. Pour into the casserole, cover and cook in a slow oven—300°F (150°C), Gas 2 —for 3–3½ hours.

An hour before the casserole is ready, scald the mushrooms and cut in halves vertically. Stew gently in the butter for about 10 minutes and then stir into the casserole.

Lombardy Pot Roast *(serves 6–8)*

3lb (1.4kg) piece of beef (not the best cut, but topside, rump or brisket)	1 onion, sliced
	2 tbsp chopped parsley
	A strip of lemon peel
4 rashers bacon, finely chopped	8fl oz (240ml) cup red wine
1 carrot, chopped	4fl oz (120ml) stock or water
1 stalk of celery, chopped	Salt and pepper

Put the bacon in a heavy saucepan and cook over low heat until soft. Add meat and turn it in the bacon fat to brown on all sides. Add rest of ingredients, cover and simmer gently for 2–2½ hours. Add more water if it dries up during cooking.

Carbonnade of Beef *(serves 4)*

1lb (450g) skirt of beef	¾pt (450ml) stock or vegetable cooking water
Seasoned flour	
1oz (30g) lard or dripping	¼pt (150ml) red wine or sherry-type wine
1lb (450g) onions, peeled and sliced	

Skin the meat and trim off the fat. Slice across at an angle with sharp knife into thin slices. Toss slices in seasoned flour and brown lightly in the fat. Lift out the meat and arrange in a casserole in alternate layers with the onions. Stir a little extra flour into the fat in frying pan, stir over moderate heat till browned, stir in stock and wine, bring to boil, strain over meat, put on lid and cook in middle of a slow oven—290°F (145°C), Gas 1–2—for 2½–3 hours.

Spiced Beef Casserole *(serves 6)*

2lb (900g) chuck steak
2 tbsp water

Salt and pepper
1½lb (680g) old potatoes

For the sauce

8oz (230g) tomatoes, skinned and chopped (or small tin of tomatoes, chopped)
1 tbsp chopped green pepper
1 tbsp finely chopped onion
1 small apple peeled and chopped
2oz (60g) sugar

½ tsp powdered cinnamon
½ tsp powdered nutmeg
½ tsp powdered allspice
1 tsp salt
Pepper to taste
1 wineglass (2½fl oz or 75ml) dry white wine

Trim the beef, cut in 1in (2.5cm) cubes, put in a greased shallow casserole with the water and seasoning, cover and cook in a moderate oven—350°F (175°C), Gas 4—until tender, about 1½ hours. Meanwhile, make the sauce. Put the tomatoes, chopped pepper, onion and apple in a saucepan, cover and simmer until very soft, about 45 minutes. Add rest of sauce ingredients and boil uncovered for 10–15 minutes until thick. Peel the potatoes and parboil them for 7 minutes. Cut into ¼in (6mm) slices. Put a layer of potato in another shallow ovenproof dish, then a layer of the meat, pour over some sauce and continue until all is used, finishing with potato. Pour the liquid from the beef dish all round the sides. Brush over top with a little melted butter. Cover and cook for 30 minutes at 400°F (205°C), Gas 7, uncover and cook another 30 minutes or until potato is lightly browned. Serve with a green salad.

Swedish Meat Balls *(serves 4)*

8oz (230g) minced beef
8oz (230g) lean pork, minced
8 tbsp breadcrumbs
¼pt (300ml) milk
1 medium sized onion
2 tbsp butter

2 tsp salt, ¼ tsp pepper
Pinch each of paprika and dry mustard
1 egg
½ cup (4fl oz or 120ml) each of dry white wine and water

Soak the crumbs in the milk. Chop the onion finely and cook gently in half the butter until golden. Add to the crumbs the meat, cooked onion and seasonings; break the egg into the mixture and stir well. Melt the rest of the butter in a frying pan, form the meat mixture into small balls, and fry until brown all over, shaking pan to brown them evenly. Put in a few at a time; when all are done pour the wine and water into the pan with them and cook gently for about 15 minutes until the liquid has been absorbed. Serve with boiled rice and a salad.

Bobotee *(serves 3–4)*

1lb (450g) lean mutton, minced	Juice of 1 lemon
Large slice of bread	6 chopped blanched almonds
A wineglass of white wine (eg apple)	1 small tsp each of salt and sugar
	½ tsp pepper
1 tbsp butter	2 eggs
1 large onion, chopped	A bayleaf
1 tsp curry powder	¼pt (150ml) milk
8 tbsp seedless raisins	

Soak the bread in the wine and fry the chopped onion in the butter. Squeeze out and crumble the bread. Mix together bread,

onion, meat, curry powder, raisins, almonds, seasonings, lemon juice and 1 beaten egg. Put in a greased pie dish and lay the bayleaf on top. Beat up the other egg in the milk, add any remains of wine, pour over all and bake in a warm oven—325°F (160°C), Gas 3—for 1½ hours. Serve with boiled rice and mango chutney.

Saddle of Lamb in Wine *(serves 3)*

1lb (450g) piece of saddle of lamb	Small wineglass of white wine
Salt and pepper	1 bayleaf
1 rasher of bacon	1 tsp flour
2oz (60g) lard	4 tbsp single cream or top of milk
1 onion, sliced	

Scald the meat with hot water, dry well, rub with salt and dust lightly with pepper, and dot over with chopped bacon. Heat lard in a meat tin, put in the meat, surround with slices of onion, pour in the wine, add the bayleaf and roast in a hot oven—450°F (230°C), Gas 7–8—for about an hour, basting frequently. Thicken the gravy with the flour, add cream, bring to boiling point and serve.

Lamb with Red Wine *(allow 8oz/220g of meat per serving)*
Leg of lamb is the most suitable cut for this dish. To each 1lb (450g) weight of meat allow:

A small fragment of garlic (1 clove is enough for a 6lb [2.75kg] joint)	1 tsp butter
	2 tsp olive oil
	1 tbsp red wine
A pinch of rosemary (¼ tsp)	Salt and pepper

Rub the meat with salt and pepper. Cut a slit on each side and insert a small piece of garlic, a quarter of the rosemary, and salt and pepper. Smear the butter in a roasting dish and put in the meat. Pour the olive oil over it and sprinkle on the rest of the rosemary. Put in oven preheated to 400°F (205°C), Gas 7, and after 10 minutes reduce heat to 325°F (160°C), Gas 3. Cook for 2½ hours, pouring on the wine a teaspoonful at a time at intervals. Slice very thin to serve.

Pork Chops Modena
For each person allow:

1 large chop	2 tbsp water
1 clove garlic	1 tbsp apple wine or cider
A small pinch of rosemary, sage,	
salt and pepper, mixed together	

Cut a clove of garlic and rub over each chop. Discard the garlic. Rub the herb and seasoning mixture into each chop. Place in a frying pan with cover, or other suitable shallow pan, add the water and simmer for about 45 minutes until the water has evaporated. Remove cover and let the chops brown. Add the wine or cider and cook for a few minutes, turning chops occasionally, until liquid is reduced to almost nothing.

Pork Chops with Prune Sauce *(serves 4)*

4 pork chops	Oil or butter for frying
Salt and pepper	2 tbsp white wine

Heat the oil with the salt and pepper in a stewpan and in it fry the chops on both sides, add the wine and cook over lower heat until wine has evaporated, remove the chops to a hot dish and keep warm.

For the sauce

8 prunes (previously soaked over- night in water to cover)	1 onion, chopped
	2 slices lean ham, chopped
A pinch of thyme and a bayleaf	2 tbsp wine vinegar
1oz (30g) butter	Salt

Take the soaked prunes and cut the flesh off the stones. Place in a small saucepan, just cover with some of the water in which they were soaked, add a pinch of thyme (preferably fresh, chopped) and a bayleaf and cook until soft. Remove the bayleaf and put the prunes through a sieve or food mill.

Melt the butter, fry in it the chopped onion and ham until light brown, add the vinegar and salt if required, cook until liquid is reduced by half, mix in the prune purée and reheat. Pour over the cooked chops to serve.

Coq au Vin *(serves 8)*

2½–3lb (1–1.5kg) chicken
2 tbsp olive oil
12 small onions, skinned
1oz (30g) plain flour
¼pt (150ml) red wine
1 chicken stock cube
¼pt (150ml) hot water
1 clove garlic

1 bayleaf
½ tsp dried thyme
4oz (110g) button mushrooms, scalded
Salt and pepper
4 slices French bread
2oz (60g) butter

Prepare the chicken (thaw thoroughly if frozen) and cut it into 8 pieces—2 drumsticks, 2 thigh and side pieces, 2 wings, 2 pieces breast. Heat oil in a saucepan and fry the chicken pieces, 5 minutes each side, putting them aside as they are done. In the remaining oil fry one of the onions, chopped, for 5 minutes. Stir in flour until browned. Remove from heat and stir in the wine. Add the stock cube dissolved in the water. Add remainder of onions, whole, herbs and crushed clove of garlic (on a thread for easy removal). Now add mushrooms, salt and pepper to taste, and chicken. Cover with well-fitting lid and simmer very gently for 1¼ hours. Alternatively put all into a casserole in a moderate oven—350°F (175°C), Gas 4—for 1¼ hours. A quarter of an hour before the chicken is ready, cut the bread into fancy shapes with a cutter, or make diamonds with a knife. Heat butter in a frying pan and fry bread on both sides. Turn the chicken mixture into a serving dish and garnish with the fried bread.

This should serve 8 people but one nice thing about Coq au Vin is that is can be made with chicken joints and so is a good dish for only one or two people. You can replace the water in the recipe by another ¼pt (150ml) of wine if you prefer.

Japanese Cold Chicken *(serves 3–4)*

12oz (350g) raw breast of chicken
Salt
2 tbsp sake (Rice Wine, p59)
2 tbsp wine vinegar

1 tsp sugar
½ tsp dry mustard
Pinch of *aji-no-moto* (monosodium glutamate)

Skin the chicken, rub with salt, sprinkle with the sake and steam until tender. Cool, then chill, and shred into small pieces. Mix together the vinegar, salt, mustard and *aji-no-moto*, dip the chicken pieces in and serve as hors d'oeuvre or with salad.

Chicken Alla Finanziera *(serves 8)*
This is the Italian equivalent of Coq au Vin and should be made with a grape wine. The Marsala at the end of the recipe can be replaced by raisin wine, tea wine, or a similar heavy sweet type.

1 4lb (1.8kg) chicken	1 tbsp flour
6 tbsp olive oil	4 tbsp chicken stock
1 small onion, thinly sliced	4 tbsp dry red wine
1 carrot, chopped	Salt and pepper
2 tbsp celery, chopped	4oz (110g) mushrooms, sliced
2 tbsp parsley, chipped	vertically
2 leaves fresh basil, or a pinch of	2 or 3 chicken livers
dry basil	4 tbsp Marsala or equivalent

Sauté lightly in the olive oil the onion, carrot, celery, parsley and basil. Add the chicken cut into 8 serving pieces (see previous recipe) and simmer 15 minutes. Lift out the chicken and put aside, strain the sauce, add the flour, blending well, and stir over low heat while gradually adding chicken stock and red wine. Replace chicken, season with salt and pepper, cook over low heat for 20 minutes. Lift out chicken on to hot serving dish and keep hot. Add mushrooms, chopped livers and Marsala to the sauce and simmer for 7–8 minutes. Pour over chicken and serve.

FISH

White wine is usually drunk with fish, and is also usually the best for fish dishes, but there can be exceptions, as for example in the braised herring recipe which follows. Marsala is also a wine traditionally associated with fish, and wines of similar type, eg raisin, are also suitable. Cider also blends very well with most fish.

Another flavour that goes well with fish is that of cheese, and a useful tip for those dieting is to grill white fish with grated cheese sprinkled on top in place of butter. Grill until the cheese is golden. Equally delicious for non-dieters.

Herrings Braised in Wine *(serves 4)*

4–6 herrings, cleaned and boned | 1 carrot
A walnut of butter | 2 or 3 sticks of celery
A few small onions | 1 bay leaf
2oz (60g) button mushrooms | 6 peppercorns
½pt (300ml) red wine | Salt and pepper
1 medium sized onion | Parsley to garnish

Melt a piece of butter in a small saucepan, put in the small onions and mushrooms, toss for a minute and add 1 tbsp of the wine, cover closely and set aside. Put the rest of the wine, thickly sliced vegetables, bay leaf, peppercorns and seasoning into a saucepan, cover and simmer for 30 minutes. Arrange the herrings in a gratin dish or shallow casserole. Strain the wine over them and add, if necessary, a little water or more wine almost to cover the fish. Cover and cook in a warm oven—325°F (160°C), Gas 3—for at least 1 hour. During the last 20 minutes or so of the cooking, heat up the onions and mushrooms and simmer gently until tender.

Serve the herrings in the cooking dish, garnished with the mushrooms and onions and small sprigs of fresh parsley.

Savoury Fish Casserole *(serves 4)*

2lb (900g) filleted halibut (or a cheaper white fish) | 1 tbsp vinegar
| 2 tbsp tomato purée or ketchup
2oz (60g) butter | 4oz (110g) mushrooms, chopped
2oz (60g) onions or shallots, chopped | 1 clove garlic or a few drops garlic essence
2 tbsp parsley, chopped | 1 tbsp French mustard
Salt and pepper | 2 egg yolks
Chopped chives | ¼pt cream or top of milk
¼pt (150ml) white wine | Browned breadcrumbs
4fl oz (120ml) water | Lemon quarters

Grease a shallow oven dish thickly with 1½oz (45g) butter. Sprinkle in the onion and half the parsley. Lay in the fish, sprinkle with salt and pepper and with chopped chives. Make a sauce by boiling together the wine, water, vinegar, tomato purée, chopped mushrooms, garlic and a pinch of parsley for 5

minutes. Add the mustard, pour all over the fish, cover and bake in a hot oven—425°F (215°C), Gas 7—for 15 minutes. When cooked, strain off the liquid and reduce in a saucepan for 5 minutes. Beat the egg yolks with the cream, add to the fish liquor, simmer 5 minutes and pour over the fish. Sprinkle with the breadcrumbs, dot with remaining butter, brown under the grill and serve garnished with remaining parsley and lemon quarters.

Plaice in Cider *(serves 2)*

2 small whole plaice (or frozen fillets for 2)	½oz (15g) butter
	½oz (15g) plain flour
1 small onion	1 egg yolk beaten up with 2 tbsp
Salt and pepper	water
1 bay leaf	Watercress and a little cayenne
¼pt (150ml) cooking cider	pepper for garnishing
1 tbsp lemon juice	Freshly boiled rice

Peel and slice onion and arrange in base of a buttered ovenproof dish. Lay plaice on top, sprinkle with salt and pepper, add bay leaf and pour over the cider mixed with the lemon juice. Cover and bake in a moderate oven—350°F (175°C), Gas 4—for 25–30 minutes. Lift out the fish, place in a serving dish and keep hot.

Melt butter in a small pan, sprinkle in flour while stirring rapidly, gradually blend in the liquid from the fish, bring to boil and simmer, with continuous stirring, for 3–4 minutes. Remove from heat and mix in the water and egg yolk mixture. Pour over fish, sprinkle with cayenne, garnish with watercress and serve with boiled rice.

Provençal Fish Pie *(serves 2–3)*

1lb (450g) cooked cod, flaked
2½oz (75g) butter
2oz (60g) chopped onion
4 tomatoes, skinned and chopped
1 clove garlic or 2–3 drops garlic
  essence
1 tbsp chopped parsley

Juice of ½ lemon
4fl oz (120ml) white wine
2fl oz (60ml) water
Salt and pepper
1 tbsp cornflour
4oz (110g) flour

Take ½oz (15g) of the butter and slowly cook in it the chopped onions and tomatoes until onions are soft but not brown. Add garlic, finely chopped, or essence, half the parsley, lemon juice, wine and water. Season with salt and pepper, simmer for 5 minutes. Blend the cornflour with a little cold water until smooth and stir into mixture in pan until it thickens. Mix in the flaked fish and transfer to a pie dish. Rub the flour into the remaining 2oz (60g) butter, add the remainder of the parsley, and sprinkle all over the fish. Bake in a hot oven—450°F (230°C), Gas 7–8—for about 12 minutes until the top is golden brown.

SIMPLE SAVOURY DISHES AND PÂTÉS

Sausages in Cider *(serves 4)*

1lb (450g) sausages
Flour
Butter

1 cup (8fl oz or 240ml) cider
Gravy browning

Prick the sausages with a fork, roll them in flour and then brown them all over in the butter, without burning. Pour in the cider, bring to the boil, simmer for about 15 minutes and then thicken and colour the sauce (if desired) by adding a little more flour and a few drops of gravy browning before serving.

Sausages Alla Triestina *(serves 4)*

This is an Italian recipe from Trieste.

1lb (450g) pork sausages
¼pt (150ml) apple wine or other
  dry white wine

¼pt (150ml) meat stock
2 tbsp grated Parmesan

Prick the sausages with a fork and place in a saucepan with the wine and stock, which can be made from a beef stock cube. Simmer for about 20 minutes, then remove from the heat, stir in the grated cheese and serve very hot.

Chicken Risotto *(serves 4–5)*

1lb (450g) leftover chicken, cut
  up small
1oz (30g) butter
1 medium sized onion, chopped
1 clove garlic
1 small carrot, chopped
1 stalk celery, chopped

4oz (110g) mushrooms
2 tomatoes, peeled and chopped
2 tbsp chopped lean ham or bacon
¼pt (150ml) dry white wine
Salt and pepper
1 tsp chopped parsley
¼pt (150ml) chicken stock

For the risotto base

8oz (230g) rice
1oz (30g) butter

1pt (600ml) chicken stock

Heat 1oz (30g) butter and in it sauté the chopped onion, garlic, celery and carrot. After 5 minutes add the mushrooms (scalded and chopped) and the tomatoes. Add gradually the chicken, ham and wine, increase the heat and cook fairly fast for 2–3 minutes. Add seasoning, parsley and ¼pt (150ml) stock, cover and simmer gently for 30 minutes.

    Meanwhile make the risotto base. Melt the butter in another pan, throw in rice, add stock (boiling), and simmer until rice is tender. It will absorb most of the stock. Combine the two mixtures and just before serving add more butter and a little grated Parmesan to taste.

Button Mushrooms in Wine *(serves 2–3)*

This is a dish where the delicacy of button mushrooms comes into its own. It is excellent as an accompaniment to omelettes or served as a starter to the meal in place of soup, or on toast, which must however be pale brown only or the flavour will be too strong for the mushrooms.

4oz (110g) button mushrooms	2 tbsp elderflower or other
1oz (30g) butter	sweetish white wine
Salt and pepper	

First scald the mushrooms by pouring over them a kettle of boiling water in a colander. When cool enough to handle cut them in half longitudinally. Melt the butter in a small saucepan, put in the mushrooms, sauté gently for a few minutes, add a pinch of salt and a little pepper, pour on the wine, return to simmering point, and cook very gently for 10–12 minutes.

Potted Herb Cheese or 'Cheese of the Seven Herbs'
This is an old Cumberland recipe, dating back at least 200 years. The seventh herb is sometimes given as winter savory but in either case the names in the order given make an easily-memorised jingle, ending 'parsley, sage and marjoram' or 'parsley, sage and savory'.

8oz (230g) Cheddar cheese	A pinch of dry mustard
2 tbsp double cream (tinned will do)	2oz (60g) butter
3 tbsp Marsala (or rich wine of Marsala type)	1 tsp each of chives, chervil, tarragon, thyme, parsley, sage and marjoram (as many as possible fresh and finely chopped)
Salt and pepper	

Grate the cheese and put together with the other ingredients in the top of a double saucepan, or in a basin or stone jam jar standing in hot water. Stir until the mixture forms a smooth pale green paste. Put into small heated pots, leave until cold, cover with a layer of greaseproof paper, and an outer layer of foil, and tie down. Use as a spread.

Potted Cheshire Cheese

8oz (230g) Cheshire cheese	2fl oz (60ml) rich red wine (eg
1½oz (45g) butter	elderberry)
	Pinch of powdered mace

Crumble or grate the cheese and then pound all the ingredients together in a mortar until perfectly smooth and blended. Press into an earthenware jar, cover surface with ¼in (6mm) layer melted butter, cover and keep in a cool place. Particularly good with cracker biscuits and mulled wine.

Pig's Liver Pâté

1lb (450g) pig's liver	1 clove garlic, crushed, or 2–3
Milk	drops garlic essence
1 teacup finely sieved brown breadcrumbs	2 eggs
	Salt and pepper
1 wineglass (2½fl oz or 75ml) red wine	Ground nutmeg
	Ground mace
1 tbsp brandy	1oz (30g) butter
10oz (285g) pork fat	

Begin two days before you want to make the pâté by putting 1lb (450g) pig's liver, unwashed, into a pie dish or basin and pouring over it enough fresh cold milk to cover it. Cover with muslin and put in a refrigerator or a cold place for 48 hours. Then pour away the milk and put the liver under cold running water for 1 hour.

Put the breadcrumbs in a bowl and soak in the wine and brandy. Mince the liver and fat together and then put through a sieve or food mill. Beat in the soaked breadcrumbs, garlic, beaten eggs, salt, pepper and a little mace and nutmeg. Turn into a well-buttered terrine or soufflé mould, cover with foil or a lid, stand in a baking tin half-filled with cold water and bake for 1 hour at 350°F (175°C), Gas 4.

Lift out the terrine, take off the foil, pour a thin layer of melted butter on top, cover with a plate or saucer and cool slowly under a weight. When cold cover with fresh foil and keep in refrigerator.

CAKES AND PASTRIES

Some recipes are originally devised for using wine, but it may also often be substituted for milk or water in ordinary cake recipes with luscious results. Wines tending to sherry type are particularly suitable for cake making, as also is elderflower wine which gives a delicious flavour.

All rich fruit cakes are improved by a little wine, and many lighter ones also. Cakes keep better if wrapped in a muslin cloth which has been soaked in wine and wrung out before putting in an airtight container.

Irish Boozy Cake

8oz (230g) butter
1lb (450g) soft brown sugar
2lb (900g) currants
4oz (110g) sultanas
4oz (110g) seedless raisins
4oz (110g) chopped blanched almonds

4oz (110g) mixed chopped peel
1lb (450g) plain flour
5 large eggs
½pt (300ml) home-made brown beer
1 level tsp bicarbonate of soda

Grease and line a 10in (25cm) cake tin with greased paper. Cream the butter and sugar well. Add fruit, almonds, and then stir in chopped peel. Add alternately small quantities of sifted flour and well-beaten eggs, stirring well. Slightly warm the beer, add the bicarbonate of soda, and stir into the cake mixture for 3 minutes. Transfer to tin. Bake in centre of a slow oven—300°F (150°C), Gas 2—for 2 hours, reduce heat to 250°F (120°C), Gas ¼ (cool oven heat) and continue cooking for 1½–2¼ hours till cooked through. Cool in tin. Store in airtight tin or wrap in foil. Will keep for months.

Old English Cider Cake

4oz (110g) butter	2 eggs
4oz (110g) sugar	5fl oz (150ml) cider
8oz (230g) flour	½ tsp powdered nutmeg or,
1 tsp bicarbonate of soda	better, ½ nutmeg, grated

Cream the butter and sugar. Sift the flour and bicarbonate of soda together and add little by little to the butter and sugar, stirring all the time, alternately with the beaten eggs. When half the flour has been used pour in the cider, whipped to a froth. Stir in the nutmeg and the other half of the flour and when well mixed pour into a shallow well-greased baking tin (7 × 10½in, 16.5 × 24cm approx) and cook in a moderately hot oven—400°F (205°C), Gas 6—for about 45 minutes.

Nicety Cakes

4oz (110g) Demerara sugar	4oz (110g) cleaned currants
8oz (230g) self-raising flour or	1 wineglass (2½fl oz or 75ml)
8oz (230g) plain flour sifted	sherry-type wine
with 2 level tsp baking powder	½ tsp lemon juice
4oz (110g) margarine	1 egg

Mix sugar and flour, rub in margarine lightly. Stir in currants, wine, lemon juice and egg. Stir rapidly until well mixed, do not beat. Half-fill 24 small paper baking cases. Bake in upper half of a moderately hot oven—375°F (190°C), Gas 5—for about 15 minutes. Cool on a cake rack.

Chocolate Cake with Coffee Rum Butter Icing

This is a simple and inexpensive but delicious cake. It can be made suitable for children by leaving out the rum and using an extra teaspoonful of hot water in the icing instead.

6oz (180g) plain flour
3oz (90g) butter or margarine
1oz (30g) powdered drinking chocolate or ½oz (15g) cocoa mixed with 1 tsp cornflour

3oz (90g) caster sugar
2 level tsp baking powder
2 eggs
Water to mix

For the icing
2oz (60g) butter
3oz (90g) icing sugar

2 tsp rum or marrow rum
1 tsp instant coffee powder

Rub the fat into the flour very thoroughly. Stir in the sugar followed by the chocolate or cocoa mixture and the baking powder and mix well. Break in the eggs one at a time and then add water a little at a time, stirring vigorously until it forms a very smooth mixture of soft dropping consistency. Smooth it into a well-greased 7in (17.5cm) sandwich tin and bake at 400°F (205°C), Gas 6 for 20–25 minutes, covering with a sheet of greased paper to prevent burning (all chocolate mixtures burn easily). Cool on a wire tray.

To make the icing, cream the butter until very soft, make sure the icing sugar is free from lumps and add it little by little, add the rum a few drops at a time and then blend well in the coffee, previously dissolved in 1 tsp hot water. Spread the icing on the cake while still soft, rough it up to look attractive and leave to set. Decorate with walnuts if liked.

DESSERTS

An old acquaintance of mine was the chief chemist of a large foodstuffs firm, and a member of that small and important elite, the flavour experts. He told me that alcohol has a peculiar affinity with fruit flavours, and a minute quantity added to any fruit-based dish or foodstuff will improve it out of recognition. His own firm used no alcohol in their products on principle but, as he said, there is no objection to any of us who wish adding our own drop of cooking wine! Here are his directions for making up an ordinary commercial table jelly out of a packet.

Elderberry Wine Jelly

Wine in jellies was a great standby among our ancestors for invalid diets. I have a charming little book, *The Invalid's Own Book*, written by The Honourable Lady Cust and dedicated 'By Gracious Permission' to Her Royal Highness the Duchess of Kent, published in 1856. It is a collection of recipes compiled, she says, to beguile the midnight hours by the bedside of an invalid relative, and the amount and frequency of the use of wine and brandy in them would make a modern doctor's hair curl. But nevertheless, one old favourite is still considered one of the best strengthening foods for invalids; it is port wine jelly, from which the following recipe has been adapted, elderberry wine being as good as port nutritionally.

¼pt (150ml) elderberry wine	1in (2.5cm) piece of cinnamon
¼pt (150ml) water	stick
3 lumps of sugar	½oz (15g) powdered gelatine
	1 lemon

Put all the ingredients except the lemon into a saucepan and let them soak a few minutes. Scrub the lemon, peel off thinly the yellow part of the rind and add it to the rest. Squeeze the juice, add to the pan and stir over low heat until the gelatine is completely dissolved. It must on no account boil. (Note—a double saucepan or a jar standing in hot water may be used here.) Set it in a warm place for half an hour, then strain through muslin into a basin rinsed in cold water. Allow to set and serve a small portion at a time.

Zabaglione

This, the most famous of all wine-based sweets, should strictly be made with Marsala, but I don't see why the penniless winemaker should be for ever debarred from enjoying something we might call English Zabaglione, since that awful word 'mock' is something I won't have in my kitchen vocabulary.

The home-made wine I would suggest for this dish is

bramble, but in any event it should be a rich and fruity one of heavy body, perhaps raisin or apricot wine, or prune sherry.

For each person:

2 egg yolks	2 tbsp wine
1 level tbsp caster sugar	

Have ready a saucepan of hot water, just simmering, not boiling rapidly. Put the egg yolks in a basin which will fit nicely into the saucepan, or of course use a double boiler if you have one. Add the sugar and whisk well together with a rotary whisk. Then add the wine a little at a time, still whisking. No need to go at it madly, just steadily. Put the basin in the hot water and go on whisking slowly until the mixture thickens. Don't let the water boil or the Zabaglione will curdle. It takes ten or twelve minutes to thicken as a rule.

Have sundae or sherbet glasses standing in a warm place, spoon the Zabaglione into them and serve hot. Ignore recipes which suggest serving it iced or adding some of the egg whites.

Surplus egg whites from Zabaglione or other dishes may be kept, covered, in a basin in a cool place for up to 24 hours and may then be used to make meringues or meringue-topped sweets. Many cakes will benefit from the addition of an extra egg white.

Surplus egg yolks are not quite as easily used as whites, but one egg yolk can be added to lemon curd; added to Zabaglione; used to thicken and add nourishment to soup (don't let soup boil after adding); added to many cake recipes; and beaten and stirred into rice pudding and other milk puddings.

Bavaroises or Bavarian Creams

These are extremely useful desserts, especially as a cold pudding for parties which can be made the previous day. They are improved by a touch of wine and can absorb an extra egg white if necessary. They can also be made more luxurious by the addition of 3oz (90g) of ground hazelnuts and 4fl oz (120ml) of stiffly whipped cream.

Coffee Bavarian Cream *(serves 4–6)*

This invariably impresses people and goes down with 'oohs' and 'ahs', but if you or your guests are anti-coffee, try the next recipe, Spanish Bavarian Cream. The curious hybrid title, like the recipe, comes from America. In most English cookery books 'Bavaroise' or 'Crème Bavaroise' is the generic title. The nearest English equivalent, milk jelly, has perhaps unfortunately stodgy and nursery-like connotations.

1 tbsp powdered gelatine	2 eggs, separated
2 tbsp cold water	2oz (60g) sugar
¼ cup (2fl oz or 60ml) milk	Pinch of salt
1 cup (8fl oz or 240ml) strong black coffee	10 drops vanilla essence

These are the original ingredients, but to improve the flavour and make it into a wine dish, leave out 1 tbsp of the coffee and replace it by 1 tbsp of a sweet white wine or a sherry-type wine.

Put the gelatine to soak in the cold water. Put the milk, coffee, wine if used, egg yolks, sugar and salt in a basin placed in hot water, whisk or stir briskly over the boiling water until the mixture thickens (about 5 minutes). Remove from heat and stir in gelatine and vanilla. When cool, fold in the stiffly beaten egg

whites. Pour into a large bowl or individual glasses or moulds. and keep in a cool place overnight. To serve, turn out the moulds and cover with whipped cream, or if in a large bowl, pour a layer of cream all over the top and decorate with a spiral of chocolate vermicelli. To serve really cold, put in the fridge for half an hour. Gelatine dishes should never be refrigerated overnight or for many hours as it toughens the gelatine and makes them unpalatable; instead keep, covered, in a cool place.

Spanish Bavarian Cream *(serves 4–6)*

1 tbsp powdered gelatine	3 eggs separated
½ cup (4fl oz or 120ml) cold water	2oz (60g) sugar
	20 drops (⅓ tsp) vanilla essence
1½ cups (12fl oz or 360ml) scalded milk	1 tbsp marrow rum or rhubarb brandy

Soak the gelatine in 2 or 3 tbsp of the water. Put the rest of the water, milk, sugar and egg yolks in a basin over hot water. Whisk or stir for 5 minutes or until thick. Remove from heat, add vanilla and marrow rum. When cool fold in the stiffly beaten egg whites and pour into moulds or bowls as for last recipe. Leave to set overnight. Serve plain or with cream as preferred.

Raspberry Condé

This is one of the classic simple sweets, and again one where a small amount of wine makes it even better.

Take some fresh raspberries and put them in layers in a bowl, sprinkling each layer lightly with caster sugar. Then pour over a little raspberry, bramble or elderflower wine, about 1 tbsp to 4oz (110g) fruit (wine may be omitted). Stand the bowl in a cool place for 10–15 minutes.

Into sundae glasses put portions of cold rice pudding, heaping them up at one side of the glass. Heap the raspberries on the other side, put a spoonful of whipped cream on top, and serve at once.

Raspberry Condé of all sweets must have genuine ingredients. The raspberries must be fresh, not frozen, the rice pudding home-made, and the smallest portion of real cream is preferable to great dollops of something out of a packet. It is actually a cheap sweet if you are lucky enough to grow your own raspberries, and is a dainty enough dish to be set before a king or even a president!

Figs in Wine

Fresh or dried figs   Demerara sugar
Sweet white wine

Wash dried figs well, set overnight in wine just to cover, add 1 tsp of Demerara sugar to each ½pt (300ml) of the mixture and stew gently until tender. For fresh figs, skin the figs carefully and poach gently in the wine and sugar for 15–20 minutes. Serve with cream. May be eaten hot or cold.

Spiced Pears in Red Wine with White Wine Sauce
(allow 1 large pear per serving)
This luxurious sixteenth-century dish is quite feasible for modern times when you have home-made wine available—especially if you grow the pears too!

Choose ripe dessert pears, peel and halve them carefully, take out the cores, and drop them into water with a little lemon juice or white wine vinegar in it to keep them from discolouring. When ready put the pears in a shallow saucepan and pour in red wine barely to cover. Add a little sugar to taste, one or two cloves and a pinch of powdered cinnamon. Simmer slowly for 15–20 minutes, and pick out the cloves before serving.

The sauce:

4 eggs   1 tbsp honey
2 tbsp caster sugar   2 tbsp white wine
Strip of lemon peel   2 tbsp water

Break the eggs into a basin, stir in sugar until white and frothy. Add strip of lemon peel. Whisk in the honey with an egg whisk, place basin in a pan of boiling water, mix wine and water and add by degrees, whisking all the time. When all the liquid has disappeared and only froth remains, take out the strip of peel, pour the sauce over the hot pears and serve at once.

136

Baked Pears in Wine *(serves 3–4)*

1lb (450g) pears	Blade of mace
¼pt (150ml) elderflower wine	Pinch of cinnamon
2oz (60g) sugar	2 or 3 cloves
¼pt (150ml) water	Juice of an orange

Put all the ingredients into a covered casserole and cook in a moderate oven—375°F (190°C), Gas 5—until pears are soft (30–45 minutes). This less rich version of spiced pears is adapted from *The Invalid's Own Book* (p132).

Three luxury sweets

Ginger Wine Jelly *(serves 4)*

½pt (300ml) water	Powdered gelatine to set 1pt
1 tbsp sugar	(600ml)—approx ½oz (15g)
Peel and juice of 1 lemon	1 tbsp marrow rum
8fl oz (240ml) ginger wine	

Put the water, sugar, lemon peel (no white pith) and juice into a small saucepan. Bring to simmering point, remove from heat and stir in gelatine. When dissolved add the ginger wine. Leave to cool, then strain through a muslin-lined sieve into a jug. Add the marrow rum and pour into small dessert glasses or custard cups. Allow to set overnight, chill 30 minutes, pour a layer of thick cream on top of each jelly and serve with sponge fingers.

Athol Brose *(serves 8)*

Another luxury, if you like whisky. This is the version of Athol Brose to be eaten as pudding; for drinking version see under Liqueurs and Sundries (p76).

4oz (110g) rolled oats	2 tsp lemon juice
6 tbsp whisky	½pt (300ml) double cream
8 level tbsp clear honey	

For decoration: 1 rounded tbsp rolled oats lightly browned in oven or under grill

Put oats and whisky in a bowl. Mix honey and lemon juice in a basin over hot water and when runny add to oats and whisky mixture. Cover and leave to soak 1 hour. Whip cream until thick, fold into oat mixture and when well combined, divide among 8 small glasses, preferably stemmed, but custard cups will do, sprinkle toasted oats on top and chill thoroughly before serving. It will keep in a fridge up to 24 hours.

Rum Chocolate Whip *(serves 2)*

2oz (60g) plain chocolate	2 eggs
1 dsp rum or marrow rum	

Separate whites from yolks of eggs. Break up the chocolate and melt it in a basin over a pan of hot water. Stir in the rum. Beat the egg yolks, stir them in thoroughly, cool the mixture slightly and then fold in the stiffly whipped whites of eggs. Put in individual dishes to get cold and chill before serving.

Oranges with coconut

With a small sharp knife peel an orange for each person, leaving no white pith. Cut across into thin slices. Alternatively, slice the orange first and cut off the rind with kitchen scissors. Work over a plate to catch any juice. Put the orange slices in pretty, shallow glasses or saucers, add any juice, and sprinkle desiccated coconut thickly over the top. Colour a little orange or elderflower wine with cochineal until deep pink and sprinkle about a teaspoonful over each dish. For children, dilute the cochineal with a little sweetend water instead of wine.

Strawberries with orange juice

Hull some fresh strawberries, put in individual glasses and pour over each serving the freshly squeezed juice of a large orange. This is the perfect combination for an unspoiled palate, but those who prefer can add a little caster sugar or a teaspoonful of orange wine or white wine. Don't add cream, as it ruins the result.

Fruit Salad with Wine

The end of the soft fruit season, when only a few strawberries and raspberries lurk beneath the leaves and the birds have had most of the currants, is the time when you may be glad of a way to make the remains into a fresh fruit salad fit for an epicure. There may be occasions, too, when you have to stretch a small quantity of fruit to allow for an unexpected guest.

Assemble what you have—a banana, one or two oranges, a small tin of pineapple, perhaps, to eke out your half-dozen strawberries, dozen or so raspberries and few currants, black, red or white. Any or all of these will do according to the number of servings required. Failing anything else for the base, an eating apple peeled and chopped or a cooking apple peeled, cored, quartered and sliced and gently poached in a little sugar and water, will serve. Divide the fruit among individual glass bowls. Make a sauce by mixing concentrated orange squash or a home-made fruit syrup, a small teaspoonful to each glass, with a white wine (eg elderflower), 2 or 3 tsp to each glass. Pour over the fruit and put the glasses to chill in a refrigerator for half an hour or so. Serve with a large dollop of whipped cream on top. Tinned cream will do if you can beat into it ½ tsp caster sugar and perhaps a few drops of rum to take away the tinned flavour. Two drops of vanilla essence per 4oz (110g) cream will do instead of rum.

At other times cherries and tinned pineapple combine well, as do blackberries and fresh plums or damsons, and in winter imported plums are good with orange and banana.

Old-Fashioned Strawberry Shortcake *(serves 4)*
This really is only to be contemplated if you have your own strawberry bed and a surplus crop at that, or else the chance of some really cheap strawberries.

2 cups (8oz or 230g) flour	1 egg
3 tsp baking powder	½ cup water (4 fl oz or 120ml)
1 tbsp sugar	Butter for spreading on dough
½ tsp salt	1 quart (1.2 litres) of straw-
4 tbsp butter, margarine or cook- ing fat	berries, very ripe
	Whipped fresh cream

Sift together flour, baking powder, sugar and salt. Mix in the butter or other shortening with a steel fork till mixture is like breadcrumbs. Beat the egg into three quarters of the water and add to the mixture to make a soft dough; reserve the rest of the water and only add if necessary. Pat out the dough on a floured board till ½in (12mm) thick. Divide in two and shape half to fit into a deep pie plate. Spread all over with well-softened butter. Shape other half of dough and lay on top. Bake at 425°F (215°C), Gas 7 for about 30 minutes, increasing heat to 450°F (230°C), Gas 8 in the last 10 minutes of baking.

Crush and sweeten the strawberries, putting a dozen aside for decoration. Separate the layers of shortcake and put half the strawberries between them and the other half on top. Decorate with whipped cream and strawberries and serve slightly warm. For non-teetotallers, add to the crushed strawberries 2 tsp strawberry or white wine.

INDEX

Recipes for individual wines are not indexed but are printed in alphabetical order on pp34–64, and recipes for herb teas are in alphabetical order on pp104–9.

Additional notes, winemaking, 27
Advocaat, 75
Airlocks, fitting, 27–9
Apple and Orange Marmalade, 83
Apple Beer, 87
  Butter, 81
  Drink, 95
  Juice and Soda, 95
  Lemonade, 95
  Toddy, 97
  Vinegar, 72
Athol Brose, drink, 76
  dessert, 137

Bavaroises, 133
Beef, Carbonade of, 116
  Casserole with Mushrooms, 115
  Casserole, Spiced, 117
Beer, basic recipe, 67
Beer, brown, 87
  Nettle, 88
  Pale, 86
Bitters, 77
Blackberry Cordial, 100
Blackcurrant Brandy, 75
  Gin, 76
Black Rob, 103
Bobotee, 118
Bottle drainer, 16
Bottling, wine, 24
Brandy Butter, 81
Brown Lentil Soup, 114

Cakes and pastries, 129
Campden tablets, uses of, 30
Captain's Cup, 97
Candied Peel, 83

Carlsbad Plums, 81
Carrot Whisky, 71
Cheese, Potted Cheshire, 128
  of the Seven Herbs, 127
Cherry Brandy, 74
Chicken alla Finanziera, 122
Chicken Risotto, 126
Chilli Vinegar, 73
Chocolate Cake, 131
Cider, cooking, 69
  Mulled, 96
Cider Cake, Old English, 130
Cider Cup, 92
Cider Punch, 90
Claret Cup, 97
Claret Cup, Cold (Claret Cooler), 91
Clearing wine, 13
Coffee Bavarian Cream, 134
Cooking wines, 69
Coq au Vin, 121
Cork, to tie down, 26
Country Mincemeat, 82
Country remedies, 100
Cream of Mushroom Soup, 111
Cuba Libre, 94
Curaçao, 77
Cuvée close, 18

Damson Gin, 77
Desserts, 131
Disasters, 30
Drambuie, 77
Dutch Rum Punch, 96

Egg, whites, 133
  yolks, 133
Elderflower Lemonade, 89

141

Equipment, winemaking, 14

Face Lotion or After-shave, 104
Figs in Wine, 136
Fish Casserole, Savoury, 123
Fish Dishes, 122
Fish Pie, Provençal, 125
Flavouring essences, 79
Fruit Punch, non-alcoholic, 90
Fruit Salad with Wine, 138
Fruit Syrups, 84

Gargle (Sage Tea), 109
Garlic Essence, 80
  Vinegar, 73
Ginger Beer, 87
  Pop, 88
Ginger Wine Jelly, 137
Grape-Ginger Punch, 94
Grapefruit and Orange Compound, 103

Herb teas, 104
Herb tea recipes (in alphabetical order), 105–9
Herrings Braised in Wine, 123
Hock Cup (Hock Sparkler), 91

Ingredients, winemaking, 9–13
Irish Boozy Cake, 129

Japanese Cold Chicken, 121

Lamb, Saddle of, in Wine, 119
Lamb with Red Wine, 119
Lemon Cooler, 90
  Essence, 80
  Ginger Beer, 88
Lemonade, Elderflower, 89
  Fresh, 89
  Old-fashioned, 89
Lentil Soup, Brown, 114

Madison Mull, 96
Marrow Rum, 70
Marrow Rum Punch, 96
Mash, straining the, 21–2
Mash tub, covering the, 19–20
Meat Balls, Swedish, 117
Meat dishes, 115
Metheglin, 67

Méthode champenoise, 18
Methods, winemaking, 17
Milk Punch, 99
Minestrone Soup, 112
Mint Julep, 92
Mint Vinegar, 73
Mulled Cider, 96
  Claret (Hot Rumour), 95
  Wine, 96
Muscatel Syrup, 85
Mushrooms, Button, in Wine, 126
Mushroom Soup, Cream of, 111

Nettle Beer, 88
  Syrup, 101
Nicety Cakes, 130
Noyau, 80

Orange Essence, 80
Orange Ice Punch, 94
Oranges with Coconut, 138
Oxtail Casserole, 115
  Soup, 114

Pâté, Pig's Liver, 128
Pear Honey, 82
Pears, Baked, in Wine, 137
Pears, Spiced, in Red Wine, 136
Pétillance, 18
Pineapple Punch, 94
Plaice in Cider, 124
Planter's Punch, 93
Pork Chops Modena, 120
  with Prune Sauce, 120
Portuguese Soup, 113
Pot Roast, Lombardy, 116
Pudge, 91
Punch Base, 94
Punch Bowl, The Flaming, 97

Raspberry Condé, 135
  Vinegar, 101
Ratafia, 80
Red Rob, 103
Rhubarb Brandy, 71
Risotto, Chicken, 126
Rose Syrup, 101
Rum Butter, 81
Rum Chocolate Whip, 138

Sake, note on, 59
Sausages alla Triestina, 126
Sausages in Cider, 125
Shrub, 76
Sloe Gin, 76
Soups, 111
Spanish Bavarian Cream, 135
Strawberry Shortcake, 139
    Vinegar, 101
Strawberries with Orange Juice, 138
Summer drinks, 85
Sunflower Seed Cordial, 102
Sweets, wine in, 131
Syphoning and straining, wine, 24

Tarragon Vinegar, 73
Teetotal punches, 94

Tom and Jerry, 98
Tom Collins, 93
Treacle Hot Milk, 102
    Posset, 102

Vermouth, 78
Vinegars, 72
Vin mousseux, 18

Weights and measures, 8
Wine Jelly, Elderberry, 132
Winter drinks, 95

Yeasts, winemaking, 11

Zabaglione, 132